EPISODES

A MEMORYBOOK

EPISODES

A MEMORYBOOK

Michael Baxandall

WITH AN INTRODUCTION BY
CARLO GINZBURG

FRANCES LINCOLN LIMITED
PUBLISHERS

Frances Lincoln Ltd
4 Torriano Mews
Torriano Avenue
London NW5 2RZ
www.franceslincoln.com

Episodes
Copyright © The Estate of Michael Baxandall 2010
Introduction © Carlo Ginzburg 2010
First Frances Lincoln edition 2010

ISBN 978-0-7112-3115-3

Printed in China

9 8 7 6 5 4 3 2 1

Contents

INTRODUCTION

'A loner,' somebody said of him. A loner he certainly was. An independent mind, who left an indelible mark on art history and beyond. A laconic, intense, shy, passionate man. I have a vivid recollection of the first time we met, in the fall of 1967, at the Warburg Institute: his gloomy face suddenly transformed by a luminous smile. In the following months we had frequent, long conversations. His shyness (but I was shy as well) added intensity to what he said. Later I attended a lecture he gave on Alberti and pictorial composition: the core of what became the last chapter of *Giotto and the Orators*. I had high expectations, which proved to be inadequate. In his lecture Michael delivered, with remarkable *sprezzatura*, a strikingly original argument. I remember that afternoon as a moment of pure joy. My dialogue with him (sometimes real, more often metaphorical) has occupied my mind ever since.

The two posthumous texts published here – belonging to different genres, but connected by manifold threads – will add a new dimension to Michael Baxandall's intellectual and human profile. *Episodes*, in particular, may affect the perception of his scholarly work. But both texts reach out to an audience potentially more numerous than the one familiar with *Painting and Experience in Fifteenth Century Italy* and *Shadows and Enlightenment*. People uninterested in art will enjoy *A Grasp of Kaspar*: an ironic variation on the mystery genre. *Episodes*, an uncompromising exercise in self-scrutiny, will immediately capture the attention of everyone who ever asked, 'Who am I?'

A question about self-identity. On the threshold of *Episodes* we find the beginning of an answer: a long, analytic, hypnotic description of sand dunes. The reader is asked (the chapter is ironically entitled 'Rules of Engagement') to compare a sand dune and its properties with a person – similarities and dissimilarities being equally significant. This exercise belongs to *ekphrasis*, the ancient literary genre that involved the precise description of objects or places, either real or imaginary. Already the close connection between *Episodes* and Baxandall's oeuvre emerges – *ekphrasis* has been in many ways at the center of his scholarly work.

Italian humanists took *ekphrasis* from the Byzantines and turned a rather neutral instrument into a crucial tool of art criticism and art history – exemplified by writers as different as Giorgio Vasari and Roberto Longhi. Baxandall repeatedly worked on this tradition. But his historical interest in local critical idioms was typically combined with a sustained theoretical reflection. *Ekphrasis* is a broad concept. Baxandall once quoted a long passage (which he called 'superb') from Longhi's description of Piero della Francesca's *Resurrection of Christ*. Longhi's *ekphrasis* aimed to provide verbal equivalents of paintings. Baxandall, as he once argued in a polemical essay, was more interested in an inferential criticism, mediated by *ekphrasis*. He was deeply aware that since words and pictures pertain to different spheres, the referential quality of the former must be problematic. But he proved to be intractable to attempts to turn him into a reluctant postmodernist. He was committed to a different and a more ambitious project: showing that words for pictures can, as it were, suggest patterns of intention and webs of causal relations.

We appear to have wandered far from *Episodes* and its opening comparison between sand dunes and personal identities. In fact, we have not. Baxandall's fascination with dunes had begun much earlier. In *Shadows and Enlightenment* he had commented upon two striking close-ups of sand (one image an upside-down reproduction of the other). He was interested in their visual ambiguities, which arose from assumptions about the light source: 'It can be smooth ridges and rough valleys, or rough ridges and smooth valley-bottoms.' In *Episodes* sand dunes elicit a different kind of reflection. A postcard with sand dunes provides a cognitive model for telling the story of a life, his own life. In the structure of a sand dune 'is deposited an internalized selective record of its own history, the lamination – though this is not what we would call "memory."'

Baxandall repeats this sentence twice. Lamination – the deposit of different layers 'of variable thickness [. . .]. Here, in some respects rather as with tree rings, lies the story of any dune.' The reader of *Episodes* will come across the word 'lamination' ('my lamination') later, in connection with two crucial encounters: with F. R. Leavis and with the Warburg Institute.

Richard Wollheim once said that Adrian Stokes had 'a powerful capacity to find in the outer world intimations of the inner.' These words could be applied to Baxandall as well – but with a qualification. The cognitive model he put forward at the very beginning of *Episodes* did not involve individuals in isolation: 'The form of the dune will normally have been deeply affected by the presence and character of neighbouring dunes.' And although dunes 'lack the consciousness necessary to any human character,' they display a series of features which include the following: 'The dune is responsive to the presence and forms of its fellows but [. . .] also acts reflexively on itself, redirecting with its own form the shaping agent, the wind.'

Sand dunes, wind, directing and self-directing forces: the description of a landscape (*ekphrasis tou topou*) provides a cognitive model of inexhaustible richness, which points at the complex relationship between a person and the society around her, inside her. Complex, and ultimately enigmatic. *Episodes* usually refrains from retrospective interpretations – an instrument frequently used in autobiographies to tame the past. Between the narrator and the ego he writes about there is some contiguity, but no complicity (Baxandall speaks of 'the human beings who went about under our names five or fifty years ago'). Gaps of memory, occasionally filled in by other people's recollections, are recorded with scrupulous honesty. The changes experienced by the narrated ego, from early childhood to early maturity, are hinted at only indirectly, through his interactions with other people.

Episodes is indeed filled with people, with names, with crisply described events (readers will discover that some characters appear again in *Kaspar*, in a fictionalized form). But Baxandall's approach is based on the *arte di levare*, on the art of suppressing crucial information to give dramatic weight to what remains. Somewhat surprisingly, Baxandall writes that his mental image of F. R. Leavis 'is unusual (for me) in being a side-view, effectively full profile.' Surprisingly because one has the impression that in *Episodes* side-views are predominant – beginning with the narrated ego. Baxandall tells us that his problem with Leavis 'is a resistance developed in fifty years' struggle not to parrot his tone of voice.' And then: 'What I wanted was a short cut directly between visual properties and social values. There is none.' The reader is left with a broken trajectory , to be supplemented by *Painting and Experience*. There, in a series of brilliant analyses, he teaches us that sermons, dancing, and gauging barrels can mediate between the visual properties of Quattrocento paintings and the social values of the day.

There are a few exceptions to *Episodes'* side-view approach. One is the marvelously cruel portrait of John Pope-Hennessy. Another, very different, is the long, detailed, affectionate recollection of Gertrud Bing (*Giotto and the Orators* is dedicated to her memory). It is also a sort of portrait, not least because of a detailed description of the well-known photograph taken of Bing in Rome in 1929, the year of Aby Warburg's death. (Baxandall informs us that his own father 'was an active photographer.') The photograph shows Bing 'looking rightwards within the picture space, not outwards left.' Baxandall comments: 'I am sure this is the person I knew in 1960.' He mentions 'the sharp edge and the candour – real attention – one loved and wanted,' as well as the 'continuous moral energy' also underlined by Donald Gordon in his obituary. Bing seems to draw closer and closer: her notes 'have something of her voice and her eye for locating the evasive, tricky and self-deceiving.'

But this apparent closeness is ultimately misleading: 'The backward perspective in which I must see Bing is elaborately foreshortened.' This retrospective glance does not tame the past; on the contrary, the time elapsed, and especially 'the remote and impenetrable first thirty years' of her life, render Bing inscrutable – even to her friends, even to those who (like Baxandall) thought they knew her well. But this living link to Aby Warburg and the tradition named after him shows Baxandall that 'the Warburg lore itself is foreshortened like one's perspective on Bing, receding into an early twentieth-century German culture one is not equipped to penetrate.'

This dense passage deserves a closer look. Some of Baxandall's writings – particularly *Giotto and the Orators* and *Painting and Experience* – can be regarded as original developments of Warburg's work. But a form of distantiation is involved, conveyed by the detached reference to 'Warburg lore.' One suspects the influence of Ernst Gombrich and his highly ambivalent relationship with the Warburg tradition. But the chronological limitations of Baxandall's autobiographical project reduce Gombrich, regrettably, to a mere shadow. For the time being, one can only speculate about their conversations.

In *Episodes* Baxandall speaks at length of his profound intellectual debt to the Warburg Institute, its library, its catalogue. An elusive trace of his ruminations about Warburg emerges from a comment made by Bing: 'She wrote of Warburg: "He moved like a man in a dark and dangerous place" and I think the "moved" is meant literally, of his gait and bearing.'

Baxandall's picture of Warburg's 'gait' echoes the youthful obsession of the latter with the Nympha, echoed in his late project, *Mnemosyne*. But for Baxandall 'gait' has a metaphorical value as well. In a passage from *Patterns of Intention* dealing with verbal accounts of visual experiences, he spoke of 'an incompatibility between the gait of scanning a picture and the gait of ordered words and concepts.' 'Gait' refers to the specific features of a movement, of a trajectory: a contradiction that recalls an early passage from *Episodes*: 'We may then become curious about such things as how we and other persons are both continuous and changing in the course of a life.' The intricate relationship between continuity and change emerges again in *The Limewood Sculptors of Renaissance Germany*, at the end of a memorable account of Hans Leinberger's magnificent works: 'The motif is a recurrent stimulus and standing guideline for the actively scanning eye and is the armature underlying the structure not of the figure but of our act of perception of the figure.'

Episodes has scholarly implications but is not a scholarly book. As the very first page informs us, it is a book born out of physical frailty and distress: 'It is an attempt to pull one's self together, self-preservation more than self-importance.' Baxandall explains that his initial project was reshaped by constraints imposed by his material: 'I had intended something more analytical, in which the pieces of actual reminiscence would exemplify types and structures. Instead, whenever I set about putting down a piece of exemplary stuff, its independent demands and energy took over. Looking back, this had been the case at least since the story of Godwin.'

Godwin suddenly appears in the street of the Welsh village where the narrator spent a part of his childhood: a haggard figure, dressed in a shabby dignified suit, mocked by the local boys. Godwin, the narrator learned, was from a well-off family; his parents had died, leaving him alone in a big house with a library, like a hermit:

'I was curious about Godwin. What did he do all day in and perhaps around that big house? Did he spend time in the father's library? Did he miss his parents? Was it necessarily sad to be a hermit? There seemed no reason why it should be. But what would become of Godwin in the end? – that kind of question. There must have been some self-projection.'

For five years or so the child reflected on Godwin, imagining an encounter with him, staging a dialogue (which the narrator includes in his memoir). A moving dialogue, in which nothing (or nearly nothing) happens.

Why was Godwin so important for the child, later for the narrator? 'There must have been some self-projection': a feeling of marginality, a fascination with a different, mysterious life. Godwin remained stuck in the narrator's memory: as a possibility, as a glimpse of a different kind of life. Was it necessarily sad to be a hermit?

'Character is destiny,' said the Greek philosopher.

Carlo Ginzburg

I
RULES OF ENGAGEMENT

1.

It cannot be unusual to find one's self incoherent, at some point, in the sense of finding one's self difficult to see as something distinct, articulated and whole. If this does happen it is hardly worrying, but we may then become curious about such things as how we and other persons are both continuous and changing in the course of a life, and what active relation we have to the human beings who went about under our names five or fifty years ago; what the credentials are of our retrospective images and other representations of those people and experiences; and perhaps even some occasional issues about how the line might be drawn between a self and everything else. These are ancient questions that we may previously not have chosen to think about – partly just because the terms have been worn so smooth by the centuries of discussion – but they can at some stage come to life.

They may do so peremptorily when one gets old. Implicated in that, surely, is a change in the relation to a physical body. As one deteriorates physically the informal liaison between mind and body, whatever it and they may have been, comes under strain. The body is detaching itself, becoming a disorderly other, and it must be watched and newly learned as from outside: age and debility have their own gruesome narcissism. The subject – something in the area of 'person', 'identity', 'consciousness', indeed 'self' – then seems exposed. (Bodies seem to leave souls more than souls leave bodies.) 'One' is practically distinguishable from the body and certainly the body seems distinguishable from one. Useless for philosophers of mind – some of them – to show us how the reality must be otherwise.

So when old people take to reminiscing it is, I think, likely not to be for the benefit of their grandchildren or for any other of the traditional destinations. It is not primarily for anyone else at all. Why should anyone else be bothered with our humdrum chronicles anyway? Rather, the old people do it for their selves, and the benefit lies in the consolidation of self that is (or seems) a product of the telling. It is an attempt to pull one's self together, self-preservation more than self-importance.

However, having said this, my own project here is not to write memoir, or at least not as such. What I am interested in pursuing, introspectively and subjectively, are types of transformation that recollected past experience undergoes and the different formats into which deliberate recall arranges itself – the genres and schemes of recollection, a sort of rhetoric of recollection. My hope is that I may come to some conclusion about what shaping pressures have been at work in producing the memory-like objects and events I have in my mind – which I believe to be related to memory but not to be simply fragments of actual past experiences incompletely or imperfectly preserved.

This will call on experience of my own in its first quarter-century or so, the period that is most remote in time from me now. In other words I must produce my own material. What else could I use? But it will not amount to a memoir because the episodes will be chosen to represent types and forms. Substantial sectors of experience – and people, places and events important to me – will not turn up, either because they are not to the purpose or because I do not want to write about them. And I must write it rather than just mumble in a chimney corner because to know some parts of my mind I need the formality of producing a text.

I am not clear how far it will remain a private paper but I want the procedural informality of the private paper. For instance, I want to be free to make excursions along byways without laying a ground for doing so.

2.

I shall begin with such an excursion – an analogy as preliminary device or emblem of some characteristics of the Self. This replaces what might otherwise be a definition of 'identity'.

For reasons quite outside this project there is pinned up to the left of my desk a postcard of sand dunes in a lurid evening light, titled: *Instant de rêve dans l'Erg tihodaïne.* Sand dunes are fascinating in many ways – the uncertainty about how far they may either be slowly creeping along or secretly renewing themselves on the spot; an uncanny opposition between softness and robustness; various ways they can make nonsense of our normal experience of distance; their storing of heat or cool; their conflicting response to light as between grain and dune, element and whole. As well as buying kitsch postcards of them I have read about dunes. But my purpose in invoking them here is to find a preliminary analogy for a particular set of properties of the personal identity and to avoid, at least for the moment, others. It is not that persons are like sand dunes: in most ways they are not. Rather it is that, in spite of the dissimilarity, half-a-dozen main properties of sand dunes resonate with half-a-dozen properties of the personal consciousness I want to keep in mind.

It is a defining property of *sand* here that its grains are of a size and weight to jump or hop along in a strong but locally not abnormal wind, rather than soar in suspension like dust particles or roll along a little now and then like pebbles. The single grain on a bed of sand may jump either because it has been caught up by the wind when a sheltering grain took off or because it has been struck by another grain descending from a jump. Though the physics of the shallow zone in which wind interacts with sand are complex, grains of the same size and weight tend finally to behave in the same way. A wind blowing over a flat bed of dry sand will grade the grains of sand by mass, and this will lead to the formation of ripples. Ripples catch grains and so can grow into ridges, which may evolve into dunes.

What then is a sand *dune*? The distinguishing property of the dune is a slip-face on the leeward side. This distinguishes the sand dune from the mere sand ridge. An exemplary type of dune, the purest type, is known as a *barchan*. (The word is not Gaelic but comes from Turkestan.) The *barchan* is the product of a wind that comes consistently from one quarter and this dune takes the form of a crescent, its surface rounded on the windward side but sheer or concave on the slip-face lee. This form is intuitively unperplexing in such conditions and one can again skip the physics.

But the crescent is surface form only. The identity of any dune lies deeper, in its interior arrangement in respect of two matters, size of grain and density of packing. The first, size, is the simpler: basically, the bigger and heavier the grain, the less it jumps up a windward slope and the further it falls down a leeward face; thus a *barchan*'s plinth-cum-rim of coarse-grained sand at the bottom.

The second variable, the density with which the grains are packed, is more interesting because denseness means firmness. The essential point is that wind-driven grains pack together more tightly than gravity-drawn grains. So, for instance, the sand that falls down a slip-face is loose and soft, while the wind-swept upper surfaces are compacted. Over time the most important effect of this is a lamination of the main body of the dune. Successive episodes of the wind-driven deposit of sand leave a succession of layers, each hardest on its top. These layers are of variable thickness and tend to a slight angle that speaks of the precise speed of the wind in any one episode. Here, in some respects rather as with tree rings, lies the story of any dune. One can see this lamination exposed when one side of a dune has collapsed neatly. Serious students wet dunes to stabilize the sand and then dig sections.

(I will just mention that a second exemplary type of dune is called a *seif* – not a Norse word but Arabic for 'sword', this dune's ground-plan being like the blade of a scimitar. A *seif* is an elaboration of the *barchan* produced by a combination of two unequal winds or, perhaps better to say, by regular interference in the work of one prevailing wind by an intermittent secondary wind blowing from a few degrees away. One might characterize a *seif* as a *barchan* that has overflowed at one end into an extension down-wind, with minor slip-face events at angles to the primary slip-face. Alternating wind directions form *linear* dunes. Multidirectional winds form *star* dunes.)

The *barchan* is a model dune exhibiting general conditions of the shaping of dunes but it is not, except in large desert regions, much seen in its pure form. The dune one finds in the tract behind some European beach, say, will have undergone transforming further experience. Some of it will be extrinsic interference – water otherwise than by dew, vegetation perhaps, animals such as ourselves, irregular wind directions – but much of it will be an extension of the same forces as formed it. The form of the dune will normally have been deeply affected by the presence and character of neighbouring dunes. These will have modified the determining local wind-flow, with huge effect. Dunes are very responsive to their environment and fellows.

Much about a sand dune is unlike a person. It comes together by agglomeration and remains, in analysis, a simple three-level agglomerative system. It is not organic and it has no mind. Sand dunes are unlikely to be lively analogies for personal identities simply because they lack the consciousness necessary to any human character. So one must get to closer quarters. Let the dune be analogy not for the person but for some properties of the consciousness itself.

Inviting characteristics of the dune then include: (1) it is, in a finite but extended life-span, continuous but changing; (2) this transitive identity lies in a unitary structure (the anatomy of large-grained plinth, angled upper-crusted layers, soft zones and hard zones); (3) in this structure is deposited an internalized selective record of its own history, the lamination – though this is not what we would call 'memory'; (4) the laminated structure is also an armature of its present stability, its firmness being one condition of the way it will stand and survive and behave now; (5) the dune is responsive to the presence and forms of its fellows but (6) also acts reflexively on itself, redirecting with its own form the shaping agent, the wind.

I shall not ask much more of the analogy than that it should resonate in the background like a drone. These are properties of the consciousness I should like to stay in mind.

3.

'This (the stabilizing lamination) is not what we would call "memory".' I am anxious not to get involved in a general account of what memory is, but obviously questions about remembering, misremembering and forgetting will arise. A couple of premises may be stated here, if only as entailing some sort of rules of engagement with the topic of memory. Others will work themselves out later.

The resources of memory have not evolved for reminiscing in chimney corners but particularly towards an ability to recognize things. What seem to me the better accounts of memory lay weight on the active and constructive nature of this. That is, memory is not reference to a record in a static, if fading, archive in which we look up our past; rather, it entails a positive updating and revision to improve subsequent recognition. In fact, to remember something is likely to modify the memory. Much of memory is reflexive and self-revising and is so not strictly to the end of reproducing past actuality but to the end of improving our performance now.

A virtue of the sand dune as emblem is that it acknowledges the active presence of the past – in the lamination – while allowing the deferment of particular complexities of the idea of human memory. In particular it encourages one sometimes to neglect, while not disputing, current distinctions between 'episodic' and 'categorical', and then 'procedural', long-term memory. The access to the past I want includes episodes and categories, and skills, in too close dependence on each other for such distinctions to be always sustained.

On the other hand, the difference between episodic recall of the once-experienced one-off event and the developing categorical generalization from repeated experience of something will be of interest here for their action on each other –[the blurring and perhaps bending of the single incident by normalization, or the modification of a mature concept by a new experience.]

I do not share the view, often asserted in the literature, that when we recall our selves we see them as from outside. My experience is that memories are not often directly of oneself but of what the self perceived or felt: footprints of the self. The identity is distributed through memory, not simply represented.

II
A VERSION OF INFANCY

I.

My early personal memory is unstructured, recollections of my first six or seven years (which, I was given to understand, were being passed in and around south Wales) are not so much few as without order. I have no idea what my first memory is and I have no reason to date any episodic recollection earlier than my fourth or fifth year, though there is earlier categorical and procedural matter about. I have some recall – glimpses and wafts – of a dozen houses of family and friends and of two schools – Glan-y-nant Elementary School (Headmistress: Miss Mordecai, nice) and then the Llandaff Cathedral School (Mr Coombes, a flogger, though not of me) to which I went on my own by bus, wearing a 'maroon' cap and blazer. I put 'maroon' in quotation marks because I have no visual memory of the cap and blazer but am sure that I learned the category by being told, for some reason in the dining-room at home, that this disappointing nondescript colour was called 'maroon'. In other words, memory of the blazer is mediated.

Of Glan-y-nant I remember most the big-windowed class-room, the coldness of the bottles of milk drunk at morning break, and being told of the murder of one of the other children in the fields nearby. Also learning the Lord's Prayer in Welsh, some of which I still retain but purely parrot fashion. Of Llandaff I remember a very dark class-room, the corner of the playing-

22

field where I won my only sporting trophy ever, a silver-like cup for the elegant distance of ninety yards, and occasionally walking home to save the bus-fare for sweets. This involved passing through territory of the vicious Llandaff North gang, through reports of whose pastimes I first heard of buggery. I went to each of these schools for about a year and the foregoing is practically all I remember about them.

(But the active attempt at recall just made has produced stirrings. I have a sense or image of rather grubby yellow ribbon or braid. I think the maroon blazer may have had yellow trimming but I cannot specify from memory how it was arranged, though I am quick to cerebrate about this, working out in the light of my experience of blazers where a blazer would be likely to have ribbon trim edges – a sort of second-level remembering.)

I feel I have a strong sense of a number of places and landscapes of those times but it is hard to characterize that sense, which often seems an atmosphere or a weather, or perhaps a characteristic array of colours on an almost non-objective frame or scheme, rather than an image. Some paintings by Kandinsky remind me of such schemes. When there is a clear or at least lively image it is often of a detail, as of a favourite leaking steam-pipe at the back of the Melyngriffith tin-plate works on the canal. The apparent clarity of this pipe diverts one from the vagueness of the whole, which is a mix of brick, metal siding, canal water, other pipes, gaps and steam I could not reproduce in order.

If I had to, I think I could list, though often not by their names, a couple of hundred individual people, perhaps more. I remember rather few actual incidents and most of them are contaminated by later re-telling, whether to me or by me. The sort of incident I am convinced I have some direct remembrance of is the winter morning the wall at the bottom of the garden was found to have fallen down in the night, but even that mainly for the issue – discussed in the kitchen – of how far frost was responsible and how far it was the horse in the field leaning against the wall to sleep, an interesting unresolvable question of cause.

Some of the most secure-seeming memories are of mental states or mental events in specific places. One corner of the garden – still strongly felt (rather than seen) as in late afternoon – was, I feel sure, the site of my pondering the fact of death. I had been told that everybody dies, perhaps on the occasion of someone dying. I accepted this but at the same time was quite clear that I myself was not going to die: that was given and I had no anxiety about it. An explanation of this contradiction, I thought, might well be that I was the Second Coming, about which I had heard, but a problem then was that I sometimes told lies, which Christ obviously had not. I cannot remember resolving this but it led to some specialized praying and a not fully confident reliance on my being given time to shake down. This is a substantial though calloused memory partly because the praying went on for some years after. But it is a memory of being in a certain state of mind in a certain place and then separately of the terms of the problem, worked over at various times.

There were friends and enemies in the street, of course, and one family of witches at the end, other people's coveted bicycles and such things, regular excitements like the Walls' ice cream man on his tricycle, and the magical sense of hinterlands, over the hills and far away, aroused by the different coloured buses running along the high street into central Cardiff from the different valleys to the north – surely standard things. But what dominates my early recall is a strong general sense of the life in our own household and here too I have come to distrust my memory.

We lived in Whitchurch, a northern suburb of Cardiff, in which city my father worked in the art department of the museum, and at home I recall constant sociability. As I remember it, there were always people staying and more people in for a meal and I would now say these people were – family apart – mainly of three kinds I did not firmly distinguish at the time.

One category was Quaker Settlement people, not all of them Quakers but all active in the settlements set up to offer educational and other support in the south Welsh waste land. (In passing, it would be easy to make superior fun of this – unemployed miners and steel workers needed other things more urgently than lessons in pot-throwing or lectures on post-Impressionism – but I would defend it. In the neglect of the misery in south Wales at the time almost any good will must have been worth something, and pottery and Cézanne is what the potters and my father could authentically offer. Along with these came other interchange: perhaps the Settlement people learned more from it than the miners but it was contact and – though I am now depending on knowledge of a couple of the people much later – gave rise to those involved becoming permanently political.) The Quaker I remember most clearly, in fact, perhaps because I did not feel at ease with him and because he was soon to be the first person I knew who killed himself, was Jim P., an edgy aesthete who ran a settlement somewhere not far from Cardiff. He also had a cottage on the coast further west where a collective-like group of half-a-dozen of us would go and stay, the Carpenters' Arms at Wick.

A more irregular category was visiting performers, again of a radical bent. I liked best Walter Wilkinson, the pacifist puppeteer, an arch but gentle man who had suffered for the cause. I remember my mother telling me (in the kitchen again, I seem to remember clearly) that Walter had been 'forcibly fed' during the war and the phrase still brings an ugly image of thick-necked warders with a sort of hose pipe, a group seen from behind, masking Walter from view. I liked much less Hugh Mackay, the Hebridean folk-singer, who wore a hooded cloak and called me 'little brother'. He worked with a troupe called the Arts League of Service Travelling Theatre, which was to my father's ideological taste.

I see from a book on them that their repertory covered a range from Thomas Hardy's *The Dynasts* to music hall sketches but I do not recall actually seeing a performance, whereas I did see and remember moments from some of Walter's. They were some-times about the house, however, as was a heavily moustached pianist called, I think, Orlov; and others.

The third and largest category was 'artists'. My father was professionally involved with a wide range of artists but I remem-ber as individuals only half-a-dozen or so of those who came fairly regularly to the house. The potter Michael Cardew, after whom I was named, was a childhood friend of my father and rather different; he came to the house too, but my main memory of him is of a visit to his pottery at Winchcombe, and of that only moments of the journey there are at all clear. Much of my sense of the artists in the house is less of the individual personalities than a sense of stuffs and activity – varieties of paper and pigments, sharp engraving tools and cold-smelling inks, tweed and rough silk, basins full of compounds. These stuffs feel continuous with objects of our domestic routine – much slipware, but wooden porridge bowls and wooden spoons that became (I felt) unpleas-antly furry, cheap but progressive smoky-tinted Czech glass, the chopsticks with which one ate salad. And some of the sense is of activity – people mixing or cutting, drawing or being drawn, assessing objects or books: and Stravinsky or Charles Trenet played on the hand-made gramophone with its rose-thorn nee-dles, which I was not allowed to sharpen with the gadget. Touch and smell seem almost as engaged as hearing or vision.

That, in short form, represents the range of what I remember in our house, though I could go on listing items. But I should in-sert here, as a special case, the patriarchal figure of my mother's father, who didn't come to the house but lived a couple of miles off. We went to him. My mother's family on both sides came from hill-farming clans in Carmarthenshire, but this grandfather had become a parson and, though I heard much from my mother about earlier years in the Rhondda valley, indeed grew up with a whole inherited mythology of a mining village called Tonyrefail, in my time his parish was in Cardiff, a large mixed area stretching from slightly south of Llandaff, down across the railway towards the docks, a tough three-curate parish. My images of the Victorian Rectory at Canton are almost as strong as my images of our own smaller house. This grandfather, a man of direct and robust goodness and a moral glamour irresistible by me, did not – I think I at least sensed – fit in very obviously with the Whitchurch ethos.

All the items and persons I have mentioned were certainly there, but what I am not so sure about is balance. In particular, am I remembering the singular as iterative, misrepresenting the frequency of things? There must have been times when we were alone. I suspect I am recalling some single occasions as multiple, or at least giving them too much weight. There is no means of verifying it all now since it is a lost world, dispersed in 1940. We left the house then, but, even more, by changing his mind about the war and going into the air force my father lost many of these friends, and I do vaguely remember hearing some of the quarrelling about it from my bedroom upstairs. (I feel I can clearly *see* two things in my bedroom: parts of the fine world-landscape frieze my father had painted all round; and an occasional light effect on the ceiling, elongated shadow-figures of passers-by bobbing on the spot, reflected summer-evening light diffracted through a gap in the curtains.) The milieu was never restored and in later years my parents had little taste for talking about it. The other side of it, of course, is that I can be sure that authentic memories of Whitchurch cannot be from later than my seventh birthday.

It is disappointing to me how little period aura is carried by objects from this culture, how little they prompt memory. I have furniture, pots and other such things, some now almost unplayable acetate gramophone records with labels I cannot bring myself actually to throw out, pictures from the house, including a study by the Welsh painter Ceri Richards (a neighbour) of my mother reading in the living-room there, but they do not carry the period mood as I would like it. There are also many hundreds of photographs, and these are a way into questions now to be faced in a preliminary way.

2.

My father was an active photographer, of the family among other things, and during my childhood did his own developing and printing. Many prints he put into albums, covering a time or place, captioned and dated, many others he put into more miscellaneous box files, and others, particularly the more pictorially ambitious mounted ones which he sometimes exhibited, into portfolios. We were all used to looking into these now and then, as a family chronicle, and some photographs became very familiar. In his later years he had a massive clearing out, on what principles is not clear, in effect keeping only some albums. Many photographs that his children remember disappeared then.

My point can be approached by mentioning Renate, which I should anyway like to do. Renate came from Germany to look after me in 1937 when I was four and she stayed twelve months. She was twenty-four, the daughter of a Lutheran pastor in Halle, a connection of my grandfather's. (The dates are not directly remembered but externally assured.) At one point in this period my mother was for a long time away in a nursing-home, carrying what turned out to be twin daughters; and at the same time my father was away for a couple of months in an isolation hospital with some unidentified fever. (Little direct recall, and remembered from later narration by others.) There was a daily maid and there were other people who looked in, but Renate and I clearly became close. She went back to Saxony later in 1938 and letters passed between her and my mother until the war, when contact was broken. But in 1996 I had word of Renate (through editorial staff of the *Frankfurter Allgemeine Zeitung*) as wanting to get in touch and I wrote to her in Hameln. She was now eighty-three, I sixty-three. Her eventual reply – several thousand words in which she narrated her life since 1938 – is explicit about my parents' odd household having played a positive part in her mind over the years, perhaps a resort in bad times, and she was upset to learn that it had all ended in 1940. Her original aim had been to get an address to which she could send a dozen family photographs of that time taken by my father, on which she felt I had a claim, and she sent these with her letter.

This at last is the point. I knew half the photographs, all of Renate and me – on a regular walk along the Glamorganshire Canal and bathing on the Pembrokeshire coast. These had been familiar and were a cheerful part of 'memory'. The others – which are half-length photographs of my mother wearing an elaborately embroidered blouse (German? Given her by Renate?) and views of the interior of the house – I did not know, and I recoiled from them. I rejected and still reject them. It must be my mother, though I do not remember her as like that, or the embroidered blouse; and because of details I have to admit that two of the photographs must in fact be of the living-room, spookily empty of people. But these photographs are totally strange and invasive, from some cold parallel world, not to be accommodated. I am not willing to let them compromise me more than they already have.

So, if my sense of the past cannot accept the photographs I did not already know, what part have photographs I did know played in constructing or selectively maintaining that sense of the past? This is more than a problem about family photographs.

The question is not just what we remember and what we forget but also how we change what we remember. For the sense of the self what seems crucial here is the reflexiveness of the process. I find this difficult to describe. A sand dune is repeatedly re-shaped by wind but that wind is partly re-directed on itself by the shape of the dune: in turn, that shape has partly been produced by previous experience of wind. The agent in remembering must be partly an incremental product of the object of the act of remembering. The consciousness would have a character derived partly from its past experience, and *a* particular memory would be an act of construction by an experienced consciousness, now. The construction depends first on the selection of cues that have been retained, which it then develops within dispositions that are partly acquired. Many of the liveliest memories from our earlier lives are likely to be those we have used to explain ourselves to ourselves – even though we may no longer use them immediately in this way. This would be better in algebra.

I should also introduce here the contribution of juvenile fantasy. I remember it was remembered by others, though not directly by me, that quite early I produced the usual cute inventions – the imaginary friend 'my sister Nancy' and the serial epic 'Mister Captain Jones's Boat', which I dictated to my mother and illustrated. Heaven knows what post-Freudian epics were under way before and beneath these: I can retrieve nothing about that, though I know I should. However, the present problem lies not in pure fantasy but in fantasy seeping into actual events and recall of them. I do not know when it began but certainly by the age of five I remember myself as a fluent fantasist and this plays a complicating part in episodic memory. I think it dried up or finished about the age of thirteen or fourteen, after which I am aware of a conscious adolescent campaign to come to some sort of terms with some sort of reality, which I shall touch on later.

It seems necessary to recognize as fantasy (or at least as having been fantasized up) various incidents that offer themselves as memories. As artefacts of their period they have their own authenticity as documents of a self; and it could be argued that fantasy will project the self more strongly through not being as hobbled by the constraints and limitations set by the actual. Further, as items in the mind the fantastic elements had their part in the reflexive revision of real events that was going on then. Because of this, they are interwoven with the actual in deep ways it is often hard to distinguish. Warning signs of fabulation are, I think, narrative elegance, particularly of closure, and interestingness in general, sometimes the presence of dialogue, and of course my own appearance in a good light.

I shall represent this with an extended episode or episodic complex of which the first part is as veridical as I can make it and the second, I am sure, is fantasy, but fantasy so old-established it has had much of the weight and effect of truth for me.

3.

In the late summer or autumn of 1940 — some time before our house was finally let to the Free French Army — my mother, our maid Carrie, my two two-year old sisters and I had gone to Radnorshire in central Wales for a while. We lived in a farm-house where we had previously stayed for a short holiday just before the war. It was a remote rolling upland area bounded by river-valleys and scarps, the terrain dark-green and light-brown, part moorland with grazing for sheep, part arable and pasture. The stone-built farms were not large, but nor were they really poor. Some of the farmhouses were isolated but some were grouped in villages, and it was in one of these we stayed, at a crossroads opposite a ragged green with a horse-pond.

For some reason I did not go to the village school: everything at that time was provisional and hand-to-mouth. I had much time. My help or participation in the harvest and later in other field work was not wished or even born with every day. There was no second milking of the cows or unharnessing of the horses till evening. Butter-churning soon lost its interest, though a fresh salty smell and the cold of a dairy come to me now with the thought of it. I could and did hang around with the village kids when they were not at school but there was some constraint here. They were civil and let me join in their evening war-games around the castle mound, but I was not one of them and both sides felt it.

Next to the farmhouse, beyond a stream and small bridge, a village carpenter had his workshop. The carpenter, a friendly bearded man with a limp, was often away working on jobs but when he was there he was a main resource. (Again, the varied whines of a band-driven saw and the feel of coarse sawdust, more meal than dust and unexpectedly dry, come strong: hearing and touch.) Perhaps he was a man isolated by his trade – or, it now occurs to me, by being an incomer – and welcomed company; certainly he was patient. Now and then he would take me on his errands to outlying farms. We went by motor-bike and side-car, timber and tools in the crimson-and-chrome side-car, myself on the pillion except on rough stretches, which I walked. (There comes an image of a stone-built farm on a slope among firs, but there is something generic and factitious about this: in fact, it may be modelled on a farm I knew later in Derbyshire.)

Still, it was with the village kids I was loitering one morning in a lane near the village when an unusual figure appeared. At first I thought it was a tramp, but evidently the local boys knew him as a local. They started tittering and crossing their eyes and making idiot noises. The man came on with a quick shuffling pace. He was carrying a basket, on his way to the shop. As he came up, looking firmly ahead and ignoring us, I saw that he was spectacularly shaggy, hair and beard surely not cut in years. He was wearing a stained tweed suit with waistcoat. (Or I think he wore a waistcoat, but possibly this is supplied as an index of general formality in dress.) Ten years ago I stood within not more than, say, ten feet of the spot where I stood when I saw what follows. It did not make the memory more vivid: perhaps the contrary.

This person walked stiffly past, and the boys went quiet, staring. Then one boy jumped down from the gambo – which is a type of two-wheeled cart – he had been sitting on, picked up a small stone and threw it. It hit the man harmlessly on the back. But he stopped and half-turned to look round, stooped with one arm raised to shield his head. He stayed twisted in this posture for a moment as if he were performing a mime of fear or abjection, and then shuffled on to the shop.

I was shocked – by the mocking, the sudden thrown stone, and perhaps particularly the over-elaborate cowering – but said nothing. The boys explained that this was Godwin, the loony who lived in White House on the south road. White House, I knew vaguely, was the one house of any pretension in the neighbourhood, an oddity in this country of hill farms. Presently I went off on my own.

But soon afterwards I asked the carpenter about Godwin. It was a sad case, I was told. Godwin's father had been a lawyer from the county town who retired here to White House, a learned man known for possessing a large library. Godwin himself had been 'delicate' in some way. So he had been brought up mainly at home, the only child, and then had never really left, though possibly there had been some short period of unproductive training somewhere. When, first, the father and a little later the mother died he had stayed on by himself, soon even without the couple of servants his parents had kept. There must be money there, of course, but house and gardens were going to ruin. Godwin saw no one now. Every few days he walked to the village shop with a written list. He could talk but was silent with almost anyone who tried to speak with him. Most of the local people no longer tried and gradually he had become something close to a village butt. Really, the carpenter thought, he was a hermit.

One would say now, and I think I had in my own terms some sort of sense then, that Godwin was a peculiar victim caught between two incompatible social patterns. He must first have been deformed and isolated by an outlandish middle-class cherishing and then left in this inappropriate community, which would be unreceptive to such a casualty. In the absence of any land-based gentry, things hereabouts were much determined by the powerful presence of a few large and spreading yeoman-farmer families and a superimposed system of exclusive temperamental groupings framed as religious denominations. He surely had no chance.

I was curious about Godwin. What did he do all day in and perhaps around that big house? Did he spend time in the father's library? Did he miss his parents? Was it necessarily sad to be a hermit? There seemed no reason why it should be. But what would become of Godwin in the end? – that kind of question. There must have been some self-projection.

It was no great thing, one afternoon, to penetrate the garden of White House to observe. I could have got in conveniently by an unlocked side-gate or even the main gate, which was stuck half-open, but my memory is of climbing over a difficult stone wall – perhaps somehow to regularize intrusion. Neglected trees and overgrown bushes inside gave heavy cover, and I made my way easily to the edge of a drive bordering an area of long grass and plantains, clearly once a lawn. At an angle, perhaps thirty yards away, was a low terrace and the garden front of the house. It was a Georgian box of a size that in a different region might have been a vicarage. The walls were rendered, once white presumably, now an uneven pale grey. On the further side was a lower stone-faced extension with stables and other practical places.

Absolutely nothing happened. I did not see Godwin, and this is really the end of the story, such as it was. But the figure of Godwin stayed in my mind and at some time or times during the next five years or so I seem to have projected the story a little further to accommodate my sense of him, or of something. Up to this point what I have just told happened, I am sure, though I have not tried to fit the language to the consciousness. *The next two pages did not happen.*

Say: A little way along the drive was a medium-sized cedar with its horizontal branches, easy climbing and neat perches. It had a good angle on the house, acknowledged by the placing of a teak garden seat almost beneath the tree, set for the same angle of view. Once in the tree I thought I saw someone moving about behind one of the windows of the house, first probably, later certainly. I changed vantage points a couple of times. A first-class tree.

And then, suddenly, Godwin was scuttling along the drive from the house, almost there before I saw him, coming with the same quick shuffle. Now there would be a scene. But Godwin did not shout. He went and sat on the garden seat below and he stayed there, silent, apparently looking at the house. Minutes passed.

Who are you?, he said at last. (The story wants to go into dialogue and I shall let it.) He continued to face the house.

I told him my name, not knowing what else to do.

From the village?, he asked

I am staying there.

So not from the village.

There was a silence that seemed to need breaking.

We have come, I said, for a few weeks.

New House Farm?

Yes.

Both of us were speaking loudly; I could not see his face. His voice was genteel but thick.

They told you about me in the village?

Indeed they had. I said: They said you liked to be on your own. I am sorry if I disturbed you.

Godwin shook his head slightly.

They told you that. That's one sort of thing to know, no doubt.

Then he abruptly proclaimed: But things you know about yourself yourself are better, just so long as others don't. Yes. I say: things you know about yourself yourself are strong if others don't.

Without turning, he put an arm along the back of the bench.

You like mulberries?, he asked more quietly.

Yes, quite.

There's a good mulberry tree off the south drive, behind the sloes. To the left as you come, next time.

He rose from the bench and at last looked up.

Tucked away, he said. He turned to leave, halted for a moment, and added: Behind the sloes.

Then he scuttled off across the grass and went round the further side of the house. A door closed.

I stayed up on the cedar branch for a little. Godwin's face, when he had looked up, had been bewildering. Inside the wild frame of hair and beard were unblinking pale eyes and very red curling lips; the man had seemed both definitely old and definitely young.

When I did get down I walked openly and primly away along the drive as if leaving after some formal occasion. And when I came to the sloe bushes I made a polite short diversion to admire the mulberry tree. It was there, a decent specimen, but the birds were already getting at the berries and there were wasps. I went back to the drive and left the garden by the main gate.

This did not happen. It is a present-moment writing-up based on old – remembered – elaboration done some time in the half-dozen years afterwards. And one of the things that clinches its fantasy character is that I have at least one alternative version, in which I go with Godwin into the house and see the father's library, sharply visualized. In fact I did not see Godwin again before we left the village, but he continued to come to mind sometimes, partly because an image of him attached itself to my sense of the words 'poor in spirit' – a phrase heard quite often in a puzzling context. I think someone once said to me, what I played with as a sort of riddle, 'things you know about yourself yourself are strong if others don't', or something like it, and I attached it to Godwin.

4.

My memories of the war of 1939–45 are a bystander's. It is strange that one should still feel diminished by this. Early on, autumn 1940, from the window of what had been Renate's room at the back of the house, I watched Cardiff docks and some of my grandfather's parish burning after a raid, but I remember it simply as an excitement like fireworks. At the end, August 1945, when the news of Hiroshima came, I watched and penetrated the meeting of shocked service people held at our house near Marlow, but I had not grasped what this big bomb was and meant. I recall many incidents between but I lacked a sense of the realities. Lying on my back on grass for what seemed hours near Marlow I watched with pleasure gliders being towed to some slaughter somewhere – not, I think, Arnhem. I could say that I remember, as I do, the business of scrambling for cover from blast and glass when one heard a V1 engine cut out – they might come straight down then or they might glide on for some way – but the experience was thin because I had never encountered or even seen firsthand the mutilation, pain and grief these things were about.

Early in 1941, soon after the episode of Godwin, I was sent to a boarding school near Chepstow, where the Wye runs muddily into the Severn. It was a decent and humane school as such places went and the worst I could say of it was that there was too much fuss about riding horses, animals I have disliked negotiation with ever since. (It was serious horsiness: the headmaster 'took hounds' after the war and his son won three Olympic gold medals for dressage or eventing or such.) I went there for the next five years. My mother and sisters soon moved from South Wales to live near my father's posting, the RAF photograph interpretation unit at Medmenham, between Marlow and Henley on the Thames. He was well suited to this work and was there until the end of the war. I joined the family at Medmenham for most school holidays but progressively felt distance. My personal affairs – my mice, silkworms and snails; the allotment on which I grew vegetables for victory; my gang loyalty to the Trojans not the Greeks; my fine or at least passionate dovetailing and other woodwork-room accomplishments; my intimacies and defensive role-playings – were now at Chepstow. Family was still dear and often missed, but felt as a survival from a past epoch.

Obviously from this period, 1941 to 1946, seven to twelve, I recall much: glimpses of objects, persons and places, often related to recurrent activity or soft-edged semi-incidents, and moods.

What I trust most are a type of moody vignette. I am alone on the platform of god-forsaken Severn Tunnel Junction in the dark, on the way back from Marlow to school, trains having been disrupted or diverted through Bristol on account of air raids. Or I am with the school cricket team as scorer, visiting another school in Gloucestershire, having lunch in their dining hall, and the lunch and the general style here seem better than at our place. Or, as one of a half-dozen boys assigned to an outlying annexe dormitory, small rooms over stables in the village, I am toasting at a gas fire already buttered bread snitched from dinner: a moment of content. Or I am waving to a convoy of American trucks on the main road in the hope of them throwing gum, cigarettes or a boxed K-ration – the last of which I never achieved, but others did. Again, at Matins on Sunday, a time of hunger pangs, a hot-water radiator has exploded during Mr Braithwaite's sermon and

Major Somebody, church warden, is valiantly approaching it to investigate, walking with cautious, stalking steps, his walking-stick at the ready, but the sermon drones on. . . . I have a hundred such vignettes from this time.

Many of them seem charged with affect of some kind. For example, one heavily charged vignette is of a moment between the two worlds of Chepstow and Medmenham. Early morning, still pretty dark, known nearby wooded hills sensed just as blacker masses against an off-black sky, and the groom Bass (pronounced with a short *a*) is driving two or three of us down the hill to Chepstow railway station in a trap, as was usual for the few of us catching the early London train for holidays. (I will note that the morose Bass – at the moment in the twisted sitting pose of a trap driver – and I were not on good terms. He had been in charge of a group of us when the malign cob I was regularly allotted ran away with me on the road, in traffic. The girth was loose, the saddle slipped round, and I cantered along almost upside down, like someone in a circus. When the creature stopped and I was disengaging my feet from the stirrups I *let go of the reins*. The cob just stood there, in fact, but letting go of reins is a quite basic error, of course, and when Bass caught up with us he rightly shouted me out for it. Also, he considered my grooming slovenly.) The image of being in the trap engages most of the senses but most of all a seen tactility. One is sitting within the low-walled square, the absurd little door at the back shut, both snug and exposed. The ensemble of varnished wood around one – low walls, narrow seats, locker, brass fittings – has a sort of spare stylishness about it, a product (I would now say) of real culture. On each side is a big slow slender wheel and these two, delicately quivering in response to any unevenness in the roadway, have a fascinating independence of each other in their finer movement. I almost am the trap. The affect in this moment is enormous but I do not know what it is or why. I think it has something to do with poise, the extraordinary lightness and balance of a trap, which one knew from handling them. And this possibly connects with my having acutely lacked physical poise since an undoctored fever – retrospectively diagnosed as mild polio – I had had in Godwin's village. I repeat, I feel as if I *am* the trap.

It is such vignettes that carry most charge for me in memory, more than narrable episodes or describable textures of the everyday. And I suspect they are the live element in both of these. But since the Godwin episode was so determined by fantasy I must now attempt one more extended narrative episode.

5.

Summer evenings were long but one still had to go to bed early, and at my school lights were put out at half past seven. For one summer term at that school, perhaps 1945, I and another trustworthy senior boy, Donovan (say), had been moved to a dormitory of much younger boys, of whom we were meant to be in charge. The infants soon slept, with whimpers and snorts, and the room was stuffy. One lacked the general after-lights sociability of the normal dormitory of contemporaries, and while relations between Donovan and myself had at one time been warm they had recently become cool. So it was my habit to go down to the lavatories and read for a time. That night I left Donovan noisily sucking an Oxo cube and went down with a book called, I will insist, *The Broad Highway*.

But before going to the squalid shelter of one of the stalls to read it, I had a look out of the window of the murky shower-room beyond. This window was long and low and partly open, and gave on to what had once been a stable-yard. It was a bright June evening, calm and quietly humming, an evening of the kind that suggests wasting it will forfeit something for ever. Living was out there and it seemed unbearable and stupid to be inside in this dark. On an impulse I climbed out through the low window into the yard – easy enough even with dressing-gown and *The Broad Highway* – and then went quickly to ground in a shrubbery that bordered a little-used back drive.

The next twenty minutes developed from moment to moment. I drifted along behind the border without any particular purpose till I came to the end of the drive, which I crossed because there was no way further there, into the beech wood where we built our huts with sticks and leaf mould, down through the larches beyond and then quickly across the main drive, into the metal-fenced and tree-lined paddock, empty except for a convalescent horse being kept there for observation. Some way off I had seen a couple of masters walking out of the school together, on their way to some pub no doubt, and the headmaster bowling along the main drive in his old Austin. But there had been no close encounters.

It became unclear where to drift further. The lower end of the paddock was all right but not somewhere particularly to go, and it had no useful outlet beyond. On the other side of the paddock were the walled kitchen garden and then, beyond a small bamboo plantation, the swimming pool, after which things soon degenerated into rose gardens and the formal front of the school. A story of Mortimer came to mind.

Mortimer was a legendary figure, expelled from the school some time before any of the present boys had arrived. He lived on as a handful of tales of havoc and daring, each grounded in physical detail and concrete location. A classic exploit had been to go down from his dormitory one evening and bathe alone in the swimming pool in defiance of rules. He had been caught and famously beaten. The question of the hero's exact route may still have been occasionally discussed, but most people would have thought of him as having gone direct, across a playing field on the dormitory side of the school.

It occurred to me now that two sides of the paddock and an obscure path along the kitchen-garden wall would bring me fairly neatly to the pool. I moved on, without fixed intentions. But once I got to the pool there was no need to ponder. No one was about and the obvious thing was to complete the operation with a quick swim. I put down *The Broad Highway*, shook off slippers and gown and pyjamas, and eased myself into the water. I did a formal length and back of quiet breaststroke, got out, dressed, took up my book, and set off damply back.

The return journey was faster and I did it in high spirits. I saw no one and nobody saw me. I got back to the shower-room window, climbed in and went straight upstairs without incident. Donovan was asleep and so I lay in bed and basked in self-approval. Nobody in my time had done this, I was sure. Mortimer stuff: big kudos. I wondered whether to wake Donovan and tell him. And with the thought of telling Donovan I came to earth.

The fact was that Donovan would not believe me. I had no proof or witness, my hair was not even wet. If I now suddenly started announcing to people that I had gone down after lights and had a bathe, no one would believe it. I was not Mortimer material nor reckoned such. They would think I was lying – something the specialized morale of the school happened to bar. Also, when I thought it over, I realized it had not quite been a Mortimer feat anyway. Unlike Mortimer, I had not set out to do it: it had just happened. I had not gone boldly direct but taken a furtive roundabout route, and no doubt Mortimer dived straight in and did a debonair crawl, not a stealthy breaststroke.

Still, it had been all right. Several times during the next few days I came close to telling someone but, afraid of being thought a liar, didn't. But, more and more, I was keeping quiet about it possessively. My knowing what I had done, when other people did not know, became a support. It became a comfortable part of myself. To tell others, now, would spoil it. What I alone knew about myself had the feeling of a strength.

6.

Something like that (run through in the mind much quicker than this can be read) is what I think I remember. That is the story I would narrate, in good faith. But how much of it is artefact? *The Broad Highway* is too pat and the Oxo cube is period colour, even though Donovan did suck Oxo cubes in bed when he had them: anything like that has to be struck out from a historical record. The representations of states of mind are of states of mind that I believe I more or less had, but they are representations and belong to now more than to then. The account of the route partly inferred sequence from known topography, though it must have been roughly so. Seeing the masters going out and the horse in the paddock might even be from another such occasion. The bones of the rest are fact, I am sure: dormitory, shower-room, excursion, Mortimer's precedent, swim, silence.

How was it that this episode survived? Partly it must be that the story has played an acceptable part in explanation of myself to myself. It was not epic but it was much less shaming and seedy than some other less shapely episodes that sometimes still muscle their way into the mind – episodes of dishonesty or cruelty or funk in particular. I would guess this one might have been brought out and handled quite often in the next few years: thus partly the element of rounded artefact. How far the silence derived from the pseudo-Godwin position is hard to know, though it does need explanation: some forgotten episode of lying claim and humiliating exposure seems a more likely origin.

I shall come back to the rhetorical character of this episode as a narration in a later chapter.

[But having got this far I find I want to dismantle the narrative yet further, in two respects. First, what I believe in totally in this story – what I am convinced I *re*-experience – is still a handful of vignettes, a cluster of half-a-dozen glimpses or snatches of experience – the stuffy dormitory that evening, the view from the shower-room that evening, the beech wood in late sun, the feel of the water, a classroom in which I am thinking of my secret one morning. These momentary glimpses, almost static snapshots, are linked into a story by rather thinner stuff – inference within bounds, knowledge of terrain and period props, authentic matter of memory but possibly supplied or supported from some more general stock.

There is something repetitive about the shape of my narratives. A story is traditionally recommended to take a trajectory 'like a well-spun iron shot to the green' – steady long ascent, abrupt steep descent, instant stop. My narratives are quite unlike this, quite unparabolic. There is a tendency to peak quite early in what interest or activity there is and then run on into an extended coda, bathetic but comfortable. The 'true' narrative of Godwin has this form and so does the fantasy narrative of Godwin in his garden, and so does the combination of the two into one. 'Swim and Silence' is of this form too. As a scheme it might be sympathetic to settling things in the mind.]

III
TRUMPETS NOW NOT HEARD

I.

In 1946 the Manchester, South Junction and Altrincham Railway was still a distinct line, jointly owned by the London, Midland and Scottish and the London and North Eastern Railway Companies, all three of them being dissolved in the nationalization of railways a year or two later. It had its own green livery and was unusual for the time in being electrified on an overhead principle: three-coach units, usually combined into six-coach trains, bounced to and fro between Manchester and Altrincham taking twenty minutes for the ten-mile trip. At the Manchester end the terminus was London Road, the big station for trains to the south, but this otherwise gave on to a bombed and blighted part of the town and people more often used the next two stations, Oxford Road or Deansgate: the first for theatre and cinemas, for instance, and the second for certain key shops. Neither was quite at the centre of the city, wherever that might have been considered to be in Manchester then.

After Oxford Road and Deansgate the train ran on its viaducts, west out of the old city, over degraded but classic ground of the early industrial revolution – Castlefield! – until the line was joined from the right by the tracks and steam trains of the Cheshire Lines Committee, another jointly owned but distinct railway. (The Cheshire Lines Committee ran trains of rickety oak-brown coaches from its own Central Station to Liverpool and, through Altrincham, to Chester, a line with a special dank late-Victorian melancholy.) At this point – that is, where the CLC joined the MSJ&AR – the train dived down through a short tunnel to Old Trafford and the Lancashire cricket ground. Then came Stretford and Sale, inner suburbs, the lines now running south-south-west alongside the eighteenth-century Bridgewater Canal for a few miles, until somewhere north of Timperley the canal curved away to make its way to Runcorn on the lower Mersey and the train soon afterwards terminated at Altrincham, a centre for several outer suburbs. The CLC continued on to Chester. I do not think I ever knew what or where South Junction was but shall not allegorize it.

Arrived at Altrincham you would collect your bicycle from the long rack on Platform One. The semiotic of the bicycle was at that time still strongly binary: hub three-speed or the showy *dérailleur*, controlled by lever on cross-bar or by subtler trigger on handle-bar; John Bull or the other make of inner-tube repair set carried in saddle-bag or pannier; fatuous speedometer or discreet mileometer; head-lamp staidly central on handle-bar bracket or down low on front fork, and so on. In fact, all I had at first was a war-time utility gearless Hercules (as opposed to a Raleigh, which was the one with the bullet on the front mudguard), no chrome and just battery lamps. But I eventually worked up out-of-system to a specialist local-made machine, a Boden, with buffalo handle-bars and the head-lamp actually down on the hub. It rusted very fast. My memory of all this is analytic and proprioceptive rather than visual, structure and feel rather than an image one could draw, and I cannot specify now what it all meant exactly, but one's bicycle could not avoid being a personal statement of aspiration. From Altrincham station it took another ten or fifteen minutes to ride home to Hale, on the edge of the 'green belt' of those days.

The three last paragraphs have simply appeared, without thought or intention, a sort of doodling preliminary to writing the next section. I have no plan for writing this next section, which ought to handle a bleak and blank period that I almost never call to mind. I have little unforced access to it and I do not approach it with much curiosity. It was a time of routines and iterative activity, also of ill-defined but real malaises. It has no shape, so I shall not delete these three paragraphs but drift on and see what wants to turn up. I think their flat generality and lack of episodic relief do register the texture of my memory of this time.

Our house was called 'One Oak', with truth since there was indeed a massive old tree in the garden, and it was four ugly storeys of fake Cheshire black-and-white, at least on the front side, though this mainly gave way to a decent brownish-grey brick round at the sides and back: about 1910. My father had bought it in a hurry when appointed to the Manchester art galleries at the end of the war and everyone agreed the house was a mistake; but for me it had the virtue of allowing a top attic storey to myself and it was mainly here I worked through my early adolescence – say thirteen to sixteen. Quite apart from their having to house me while I did that, it was a difficult time for my parents, as for most people. They were tired and hard up, and there was a life, even a family, to reconstruct. My father had developed a stomach ulcer during the war and was soon publicly at odds with the Manchester city councillors over 'modern art' and such matters. My mother set herself to make something of the hideous house and to provide for us and the people who again seemed to be continually staying with us, some of them pre-war friends but some more recent. No one but I had any need for the warfare I now waged with my father. Yet we were a close, even if mutually reticent, family and I loved them all four – in spite of everything (as I might have said at the time). But this was not special to that particular moment.

The dreariness of common father-son antagonism bulks large and accusingly in memory. To some extent both of us were mak-

ing our way back into the family after the last five years. He behaved well and I did not. He was a shy and ardent man of enthusiasms he urgently needed to communicate – a Methodist temperament, I have thought – and this made him vulnerable. Along
with standard sulks and rudeness I could easily evolve a set of
poses to rile and embarrass him. Politically I postured away to
his left: I hear myself rawly ranting on to his favourite Yorkshire
cousin about the immorality of trading in wool futures, when the
man was bound to trade in them for the regular purpose of laying
off risk in his wool-carding business. Or (an easy line of attack)
I could make a point of liking music my father had reason not to.
I recall going demonstratively off on my own, by the MSJ&AR,
to the Palace Theatre in Oxford Road to hear *Lohengrin*, in the
event a comically bad production in which fat people dressed in
powder-blue were forever processing slowly in a circle, as in a
German theatre foyer. It is typical that I was fighting foul. I knew
very well that his antipathy to Wagner came from having been
drilled in the operas beyond endurance by his own father, who
had annually taken his family through the piano-score of *The
Ring* in preparation for their annual pigrimage to the real thing,
that no hint of a motif then be missed. I had analogous poses on
other matters and some stayed with me as permanent deforma-
tions. It was petty, shabby and shaming.

Covertly I was acquiring tastes I often selected and adapted from his tastes and some of the time we communicated, except that it was rare to break out of a reciprocal reserve. Early
on, I suppose in an attempt to get us on terms, he took me to
north Wales for a week's rock-climbing, something he loved,
and though this went awry I remember it as one of our better
patches. It was early spring weather, sun and snow showers, and
the first day was brittle, with lessons in rope management and
then me falling safely off or simply stalling on some easy climbs
on Tryfan. The second day he, but not I, was asked to join a

search party for a solitary climber missing on Lliwedd and he was unlucky enough to be the one to find the body, at the foot of the north face and much mutilated. The outcome was that we spent the next four days not seriously climbing but walking and scrambling over the Glydyrs and other mountains in an unusually relaxed way. I was sorry about his unpleasant experience and behaved gently, and he was less shy and talked about life. I regret I could not keep this level of humanity up.

For five years – 1946–51: thirteen on – I went by way of the MSJ&AR to school. To do so I reversed the journey already described, getting out at the Oxford Road station. I then crossed Oxford Road itself, walked along the tow-path of the Rochdale Canal and caught a bus taking me some way south, beyond the sad barracks of the infirmary and the university, out to the detestable Manchester Grammar School.

Most people dislike school but reasons vary. My basic problem with the Manchester Grammar School was that so many of the boys were so much cleverer than myself. At Chepstow I had got by respectably for five years without strain. Arriving here, a couple of years later than the main entry, I now found myself something like twenty-seventh out of thirty in Three Alpha and it was a shock I never got over. There were boys here – Goldstone! Jones! – with minds of a quite different order, unmistakably so; and, somehow worse, behind them was a crowd of normal strong talents with a quick and tidy competence I knew I could not reach and never did. Still, it is the school I remember detesting, not them or even individual masters, with a few exceptions. No doubt there were good things about it – the unusual three-week vacation at Whitsun and the subtle speedy game of lacrosse are what I can recall at the moment – and no doubt there were fine activities I quit the place too promptly at 3.45 to notice. But I still see it as what it was often accused of being, a shrivelling crammer too geared to tables of examination results. Perhaps I was there at a bad time: certainly I have met people who, at an earlier or later period, liked it. I simply remember very little about the Manchester Grammar School. (One thing I do remember is the High Master drawing a graph on the board to show us how we were the top something percent of the population. The subject was Divinity and the topic Plato's Guardians.)

The journey there from home was a lopsided V and in summer I could vary things by crossing or closing the top of the V and going direct by bicycle. It took an hour and a half, as long as the usual journey, but it had its satisfactions and one of them was to get a different sense of the grain of Manchester. The usual way by the MSJ&AR was a radius in to the old centre and afterwards another radius half-way out again: but this summer alternative was more like half of a chord and its section across the grain did not involve the eighteenth- and nineteenth-century grandeurs and clear historical line of the other. It was through complex mixed territory – outer suburbs, occasional new light industries, undeveloped but doomed green areas, blighting by-passes, villages and small towns sinking into housing estates. And part of its meaning lay in the intricacy of route-finding and the variety of possible routes. It was a chart or model of the 1930s, which I thought of as my period, romantic in its way.

What I meant by 'romantic' – certainly an important private value then – is elusive to me now. It included peculiar things: disused cotton mills specifically in strong sun; certain kinds of small urban pub and the people going into them; buses seen passing at night and the people in them; certain kinds of bend in a road or slope in the terrain. I think it developed to fill a gap left by the sudden withering of fantasy. It may have been a transformation of fantasy, a shift towards attaching the sort of feeling formerly put into invention to actual things; perhaps even a continuation of fantasy but with stricter rules about its application. I remember very distinctly indeed worrying whether the appeal of ro-

mantic things would have staying power or whether I was invest-
ing in something that would some day leave me flat. A formula
for the romantic I learned later – the ordinary made strange, the
strange made everyday – is compatible but too undefined. What
was deeply involved was rapprochement with the reality of what
was there in Manchester.

My visual sense of this was disciplined a little by an air-force
friend of my parents. Bill Colebrook was a professional photographer, a small, quiet man independent enough to photograph
only what he wanted to, which was mainly industrial landscape.
On northern sorties he stayed with us and I picked up from him,
often indirectly, a sort of visual grammar of the industrial revolution. One could learn much just from watching and hearing
him go through his negatives and contact prints but I particularly
remember a day when I tagged along on a trip he was making to
Liverpool, to do something about the dock architecture before it
was too late. We spent the day working along the wharves, Bill
(whose real first name was Avery) silently absorbed, I watching
as he wrestled with the problems of the strip-like array of ware-
houses and the perpetual overhead railway. He was in fact a very
un-romantic photographer for the time, no moody Bill Brandt
lighting at all but a Bauhaus or Moholy-Nagy alertness to angle,
intersection, and implicit projection. It was a loss to me when Bill
fell out with my parents (about a loutish South African companion he brought along with him one time) and stopped coming.

Through him I may have developed a little muscle in my address to the disused mills but at the heart of the romantic was a
selective historical past and here I was fortified by observing another wartime friend of my parents. James Owen Mahoney was
a surrealizing American painter and a sort of premature postmodernist. The eventual monument to this was an extraordinary
poly-pastiche house he built above Lake Cayuga near Ithaca,
where he taught at Cornell, but I did not see this till thirty years

later. In the late 1940s he seemed eccentric and he always was a glamorous figure to me, arriving the first time in a scarlet MG he had just collected from the factory, and always setting about obsessional enthusiasms. One was stripping and bleaching all wood surfaces in our house, which did lighten the atmosphere, though there turned out to be a long-term problem about neutralizing the bleach. A little later another was locating and acquiring the great sub-baroque porcelain stove seen in the background of Valli's apartment in *The Third Man* (1949). His pursuit of this stove – at first the original, later the drawings for a replica (which turned up in the Ithaca house) – was an epic of high-spirited persistence. What fascinated and encouraged me in Jim Mahoney was the serious playfulness, a romantic quality in itself, directed towards the past. He seemed to endorse my own self-indulgent exploitation of disused mills in sun.

Somehow implicated in all this was a sense of lost personal past. One poem I wrote towards the end of this time began: 'Trumpets now not heard I once heard / distantly . . .'. It went on to remembered autumn beech woods above the Glamorganshire Canal. Note the throb of 'nów nót heárd' and the bravely bitten-back *d* of 'dístantly', all of which I would be in a position three or four years later to place as 'plangent' in a very bad sense. I assume I stole the line from somewhere but it sums one side of things up. There had been a Fall. The Fall was presumably puberty and intrinsic, but an incident on the MSJ&AR did become involved with it in my mind.

The incident is so ordinary that it seems absurd to be giving it a prominence here proportionate with what I think it then had for me. I had been, on a hot day during my first summer in Manchester, 1946, to an important model shop in Deansgate called Tyldesley & Holbrook and then caught an early afternoon train at Deansgate station to go home. There was just one man in the compartment, fat, middle-aged, sweating and drunk. I soon saw he was fondling his penis and he caught my eye and asked if I would like to see. He produced it anyway, gross, purple and glistening, and coming across to sit next to me urged me to touch it and said we should compare it with mine. He set to groping and I fought back. I have no real recall of quite how far he got but the struggle cannot have lasted much more than a minute or two before he suddenly stopped, re-ordered his dress, went back to his place, and made some remark about having a joke. The train halted at a station, I do not remember which, and I got out unhindered by him and waited for the next train. It was a minor incident, unconsummated – as indeed it was fairly sure to be on the MSJ&AR simply because the trains stopped so often.

A trouble was that over the next couple of years I would en-counter the man now and then, usually joshing beerily about with a bunch of youths older than me in Altrincham station fore-court, where he hung around. Sometimes he saw me and would go blank-faced and turn away. He did not try anything again. I told no one about it for years after – didn't know how to – but, for whatever reason, it hung over me. I do not, in fact, think all paedophile approaches need be destructive. I had had an in some ways more intimate encounter with a master at Chepstow; that had been uninvasive, from a man I liked, fortifying in its way and hardly thought about afterwards. The outcome of the MSJ&AR incident, on the other hand, was not quite the sense of guilt reported as common after fully achieved assault, though I felt dirty: it was revulsion from the human body in general, a re-vulsion from flesh which persisted for years. Of course the inci-dent was not the simple cause of this malaise; rather, it may have been that a turn of adolescence crystallized in the course of my brooding on this incident and was coloured by it. And it served as an explanation of myself to myself at the time.

The malaise could come out in perverse ways and I recall one episode with mixed embarrassment and pleasure. In the spring of 1947 the family was for a week or two in the west highlands of Scotland, staying near the then almost deserted great sands of Morar, and one morning my sisters and I had been bathing off the sands, I naked simply because I had not brought bathing gear on what had begun as a grey day and only later became hot. I went up into the dunes afterwards on my own to dry in the sun, and when my father eventually turned up to call me for lunch I put on a display. Since he as usual had a camera with him I danced now on the sand slopes, leaping about to fascinate him with the visual interest of my body. It was an exhibitionist bid for attention, no doubt at all, but I am clear it was more urgently a bid for acknowledgement of my being wholesome, even now after the defilement he didn't know about. In short, though the logic is odd, I was determined my father should want to photograph me naked as a certification of my still being all right.

Most people, I take it, experience some version of the man in the train and often much more severe. It seems to me hard to distinguish, within the whole brew of adolescence, between a general symptom of the condition and the result of a particular contingency, partly because some of the particular contingencies are so very commonly encountered. A question then is how far a local or particular bit of one's experience has an individuating effect; and how far, on the contrary, differing experiences are funnelled into being just generic stimulations of some standard development. How finely differentiated is external determination of the self? It would perhaps be good to have more about adolescent sexuality at this point but there is pathetically little to say. I was a youth who did not masturbate and paid for it with worrying wet dreams, not understood. My preferred occasional titillation was not flesh and blood but a volume of shifty life drawings by Eric Gill – a nauseating abstracting mix of sensual and sentimental. I felt in later years that what might have met the immediate case at this time would have been a light-touched seduction by a middle-aged homosexual of a specific ironic kind (of whom I have known and liked a number) and I am sure there was homoerotic business to work through. There were friendships but no seductions. It is too late in the day to analyze all this now or to want to, but it bears mention more as being a blank than as a perceived problem.

Anyway, much brooding was done in the attic of 'One Oak'. The attic was mine, in effect, and here I retreated at six or seven each school day with a couple or more hours of work to be done for tomorrow, the vacuous exercises that made up a classical education at the Manchester Grammar School: prose and verse composition in various styles of Latin and Greek, and translation of great books addressed solely as suppliers of lexicon and syntax.

Somewhere in my brain that attic exists not just as a remembered place but as one arrangement of mental life. I cannot summon up a very clear image of all the attic, nothing like a photograph, but the plan of it is something, or is part of something, in which I suspect I still move. It is a little like a medieval diagram of the chambers of the mind, but not on the medieval system of faculties, just a simple diagram of process.

To get to it, you first went up steep bent stairs past a window with a view down past poplars to an overgrown and unbuilt-on house lot next-door and these stairs led to a landing with four doors. You were now a storey away from the people. The door on the left was the boxroom, a small room with a mean low window. Boxes and so on were usually kept in the basement, not here, and I think of this room more as where I put things I wanted out of the way, often the debris of unsuccessful or incomplete striving. It was a sort of limbo. For example, there was a small hand-loom. I had been outraged to be given this by my parents at Christmas when I had indicated, tactfully but clearly, that I needed a new bicycle to replace the utility Hercules; and since I could not very well just throw the loom out I put it in here.

(This hand-loom did have a short period of recall a couple of years later when I found that one could quickly weave flash neckties on it. The school did not have a uniform at that time and some dapper contemporaries were coming in bow ties. As a counter-statement a range of handwoven ties worn with, say, my natural corduroy jacket seemed right and I first wove a quite sober four-in-hand in yellow and pale grey. This was admired in my circle but not by Rupert Simkins, the head of the classical side, a mild and probably decent man with whom I could not get on. For me he stood for all I hated in the specialized linguistic virtuosity of the Classical Sixth, into which I had drifted by then. And for Rupert Simkins I was not just a weak pupil but, as he said publicly, one of the 'silliest' people he had ever known – this from a man who cut a pack of cards, incessantly shuffled, to fix which of us would translate next; and who rewarded prowess in translation with a foreign postage stamp from a tobacco tin on his desk. 'Take a stamp!' So I set out to irritate with bigger and brighter ties, but the game soon faded and the loom was put away again.)

On the right was the bathroom, a courtesy title. My father referred to it as the dark room and once or twice used it as that. It was a grim room in which only limited cleansing functions went on. The main trouble was the bath-tub itself, already stained and pitted, and now blotched with unstable patches of white. Exactly what happened to Mr. Pooter had happened to me here: a special enamel claiming to renew the surface of bath-tubs oozed off when it met hot water. For serious purification one must leave the upper zone and go down among the people.

Straight ahead was the main room where I slept, worked at my desk, read and listened to my wireless. (This was a wartime wood-encased object that could be remote-controlled from the bed through a system of strings.) The room was a big and beautiful attic room in which the left half of the ceiling sloped down to

near table-top height. On that side a dormer window looked out
on a row of houses and on the far side another window looked out
on the great Oak. The positions of bed and desk, chair and book-
cases varied restlessly from time to time, and so did the pictures,
except that one constant was a large map of Manchester and its
surroundings on the wall to the right. I had meticulously painted
the room myself – the big right-hand wall white, the three others
a very pale sienna, the ceiling and slope a very pale blue.

This blue came near to being emblematic of the room as site
of conflict between the real and the idea, taking these terms in a
very broad, say Fichtean, sense. I had chosen blue because 'blue
recedes' but, though I repainted the ceiling and slope at least twice
to make the blue even paler, it did not recede but insistently advanced. I was struck by how my parents' friends, sent up to see
what a good job I had made of my room, always commented on
the cleverness of using blue for the slope, because (as they pointed
out) blue recedes; yet anybody could see that here it did not. Reality with its complications, facing white wall and dormer window
and visible surface, was just too strong. This was so of much that I
addressed here as I tried to match what I read with what I saw – for
instance, the novels of Dornford Yates (borrowed from the local
public library) with life in Manchester now.

However, the fourth room, between the main room and the
bathroom, was a place of more autonomous Mind. It was much the
same size and shape as the main room except that it lacked the dormer window and was darker. When I arrived in 1945 I had thought
of building a model railway there and had got as far as constructing
a baseboard along two sides and buying three eighteen-inch sections of track to use as modules. It got no further than this, since
money and will gave out. But for some time the three modules lay
on the baseboard and I pondered possibilities, projecting in my
mind possible circuits of track running throughout the room and,
even more, the landscape and buildings that would go with them.

After a while my mother took to storing apples on the baseboard and I removed the modules to the boxroom, but a habit of going into the railway room (as it was ironically known downstairs) for the purpose of brooding on things survived and now went beyond circuits of track. The emptiness and dimness and the smell of the apples – many of which I ate – were all pleasant, and here I both imagined and reflected. I am not sure how far I even needed to be in it physically to be in it functionally; it may have encouraged the schizoid impulse of adolescence but on the other hand perhaps having an external and material brooding place made it less necessary to excavate an interior one. I do not know which.

(There were other complementary parts of the topography of Mind, elsewhere. The most powerful was the Derbyshire moor called Kinder Scout, in the High Peak: the family spent several summers in a borrowed cottage below this, my father getting in to work by train from Hayfield. Kinder Scout is a plateau two thousand feet high and a couple of miles across and I spent many days on it alone, walking or reading or pondering. The top is a great labyrinth of peat hags, ponds and streams in deep trenches, and once inside this there is no outlook; but at its edges the outlooks from sandstone crags are grand, some with bizarre groups of monumental rocks below them, and a few waterfalls or downfalls, one of which in a west wind notoriously seems to go up rather than down. This territory invited allegory, much (I later recognized) in the style of a French baroque allegorical landscape – the realm of this or that. It was a sort of formatted blank into which I could project changing meanings, and then enter.)

I was solitary in the attic, not lonely: I had friends at school but certainly did not want them to come here. I resisted initiatives from my parents, or more often from friends of my parents with offspring, to have me spend time with others of my age; I read a lot. If I got bored I went out on my bicycle or – more and more as time passed – went out to learn Manchester.

Manchester was intriguing. I had some feeling for the history of the place and also some sense of what the Germans call *Manchestertum*. I had not read Engels but I knew roughly who he was. Late after-images of *Manchestertum* could still be glimpsed: for some reason I was ceremoniously taken to lunch at the Manchester Reform Club itself – difficult lamb cutlets – by the elderly and interesting Sir Thomas Barlow, an astringent Liberal mill-owner and Dürer scholar; and there were one or two less idiosyncratic old-Liberal grandees out in Didsbury and beyond who gave parties for 'young people', which I once or twice braved in order to make quite sure I did not want to go to them.

To my eye the town had its high culture. *The Guardian* was still *The Manchester Guardian* and still had roots, and (this is not really to change the subject) the Hallé orchestra was in its Barbirolli prime, before the blurring enlargement – from six basses to eight and so on in proportion – that went with the move back later to the bombed and rebuilt Free Trade Hall. In my time it played in a very small hall with very uncompromising wooden reflecting surfaces and my memory of the first half of the first concert I heard there, Rossini and Bizet, remains a standard of sheer thrilling human brilliance, brave and clear. In another small hall down in Deansgate the then BBC Northern Orchestra at least enlarged my range. (I scrounged permits to sit in the little gallery when they were recording for broadcast, though the strongest memory there is the horror of witnessing the firing of a drunken flautist for not having prepared his solo part in a piece called *Pastorale*: he had settled for vaguely bucolic riffs of his own which enraged the composer Bliss, conducting. I still dream about this, of course in the role of the unprepared flautist.) I also developed a taste for the old-fashioned second-hand bookshops in and around John Dalton Street; at first I was in search of classical texts and cribs, *Kelly's Keys* (to the Classics) and *Bohns*, but that led on. All this was within the half-mile square between the Central Library and Deansgate.

The real challenge was in the mucky physical fabric of the larger town, the nineteenth-century structures on the often hidden eighteenth-century groundwork, and this was baffling. With its contradictions between a sort of ruthless reason and sheer mess, and between strange local magnificences and the surrounding clinker from old spent energies, it was hard to grasp. I do not think I even had it arranged into oppositions like this. Rather, the place presented itself and still comes to mind as a sprawling labyrinth of obsolescent industry and meanly housed commerce, almost deserted canals and capricious wandering railway lines, dire slums and near-slums and snug burgess reservations, county-town classicism and the gigantized pseodogothic of the town hall and the university – all this clearly with a mature or at least established human organization. I was curious about the lives of people here. Many of them, I suspected in some moods, were romantic, but in other moods I recoiled into a thin pastoral fantasy and went home to listen to early Vaughan Williams.

When, years later, I read Leon Battista Alberti's great treatise *On Architecture* I realized that one way of understanding Manchester is to adapt his fifteenth-century sense of buildings as many-dimensioned moral behaviour within a class-coded public/private functional system, but I did not know Alberti then. A local juxtaposition like that of the superb train-shed of the then Central Station (Cheshire Lines Committee), the mean unfinished approach to it, and the neo-whatever Midland Hotel nearby needs more careful analysis than the showy contrast on its own suggested. There are conflicting layers of system here: the structurally clearheaded Station had been an unnecessary station – a folly of capital – but, given the Station and its site and the system, the grotesque Hotel had point and great success.

The winters of the late 1940s, before real smoke abatement, saw the last great nineteenth-century fogs in Manchester, days spent moving slowly through muffling vapour, and I am glad to

have lived this old metaphor, though I am not up to conveying
here the fog's sheer sublimity and command. Summers were sul-
try and featured droughts and cricket. I longed to be a very crafty
very slow bowler and spent hours trying to flip controlled leg
breaks and googlies to the Oak at home. But I also spent time at
the Old Trafford cricket ground, during term dropping in there
for a free hour or two on the way home sometimes, in vacation
spending whole days. They played the old county game here,
exclusively three-day matches, amateur captains, some of them
clownish, and a diversity of subtle slow bowlers still. To be there
at 11.30 on the second day as they came out, six hours of it ahead
today, five and a half tomorrow, and Lancashire notorious for
drawing its matches, was participation in a high Victorian rite.
The stands at Old Trafford were also a place for exchange with
fellow-Mancunians, since there was much time for conversation.
I did not attach my identity to Lancashire because the family
ties were with Yorkshire but I did see myself as, in terms of the
English at least, northern and I wanted to assimilate. Sports talk
is a neutral substratum on which other more difficult kinds of
communication can ride: one spent hours here with people there
might otherwise have been no unstrained occasion to talk with.
Old Trafford (like the wards of the Manchester infirmary, where
pontoon played the part of cricket) socialized and acculturated a
little, though hardly enough.

(I have just checked hours of play in my only copy of the
Wisden Cricketers' Almanack, which is for 1948, and am astonished at how its nine hundred pages bring to life knowledge not
touched for fifty years. A hundred or more names of often not
particularly distinguished players bring what seem sharp images
of the men, sometimes a face, sometimes an angle of cap or a
way with shirt sleeves, most often a bowling or batting action
or stance, only occasionally a particular incident. Howorth (R.)
of Worcestershire, for instance, whom I can't have seen often

and certainly have not thought about for half a century, has a clearer image than some colleagues I later worked with closely for years. It convinces me that there is unstirred deep deposit in memory, latent and not revised by use, not in any way suppressed but simply unneeded. How much of one's head is taken up by this? However, there is something brittle and potentially fugitive about the images which may come from them not having undergone the process of revision an intermittent recall would have entailed. I wonder whether they will now quickly fade, or crumble like a mummy exposed to air.)

2.

Manchester, or this synthetic sketch of days there, 1946–9, is petering out. I shall not attempt to prolong it, or to cover the second half of my five years there, which I remember almost nothing about. That is mainly a blur that went on too long. I shall skip to the next phase of my education.

At MGS, in fact, after two years grind in Three Alpha and Remove Alpha, I drifted into the three years of Classical Sixth but now considered myself *hors de concours*. I had soon decided that I did not want to go to a university since it would mean more of this sort of thing and, though that opened up uncomfortable questions about what actually to do for a living, it let me settle for less effort within the curriculum. I had developed a mild interest in typography and thought I might become a printer and it was arranged that I should be apprenticed to a printing firm in High Wycombe. But rather late in the day the printer – prevaricating? prompted? – offered that after all I would be more use to them if I went to a university first. I had won some minor school prize in English, on what basis I cannot remember, and now took the line that I would go to a university if I could do English literature, something that seemed appropriate for a printer but which I really knew nothing about as a subject for study.

A knowledgeable friend of the family told me there were two sorts of academic English studies: I should read Maurice Bowra's *The Heritage of Symbolism* and F. R. Leavis's *Revaluation* to see what they were like and then follow my taste. I did so and naively wrote off to Downing College at Cambridge proposing myself. I was told Greek and Latin were not a qualification for the Downing English school, which anyway had its own entrance exam for which anyway I was too late; but on the basis of my examination chits I could have a place in classics (which was an undersubscribed subject) with the possibility of changing to English after a year, or perhaps two. In the event I changed after a term: Cambridge first-year classics seemed just the same stuff I had been doing two years before at Manchester and I could not bring myself to go on with it. It was a genuine seizing up, not staged, though I was quite ready to tell people about it. I appealed to the college and to Leavis, and after a meeting with him he ruefully let me in. I must say that I got into the Downing English school through a back window.

I had liked the leanness of *Revaluation*, as well as the type, roughish paper, rust-brown binding and spare dust-jacket design with their good 1930s Chatto feel – whereas *The Heritage of Symbolism*, which I still have, I still find repellent, font and text and shiny maroon case – but I had had little sense of what was going on here. When I was let in and started going to classes I kept my head down but was excited, not having realized at all that one could read so actively. I picked up some of the lore from friends who had been reading Leavis and the *Scrutiny* group for years at school, but the formal training was mainly through Leavis's classes, several mornings a week, and through writing essays for supervisors. One did not go to university lectures much, except occasionally to see what so-and-so was like.

But since he later had a rough ride with Leavis, I wish to say that the person who bore the first burden of my elementary education was Harold Mason, at that time Leavis's assistant at Downing. It was for Mason we were writing most of our essays, and in the weekly hour alone with him matters that shouldn't have had to be pointed out could be pointed out. 'You know, you don't *have* to start your piece from a general maxim: as you're dealing with *a* book it might even be better to open the show with *a* point about it.' I left his house every week squirming with embarrassment about my own crassness, but with lessons learned. People either liked Mason or they definitely didn't: the irony and circuitous pseudo-tact alienated some, and it is noticeable that his ornate manner does not work well in print. For me he was a huge piece of luck. As he himself was someone with a classical education, even though the more expansive Oxford Greats, he knew what I was coming from and had the good nature to be patient with my gaucheries but, however indirectly, make them plain to me. His interests in Renaissance humanism and in the cultural environments of poetry were intriguing and I first read Italian at his Dante evenings. I liked his obliqueness and aggressive slyness: after a lecture by Henri Fluchère on French classical drama, 'I am wondering . . . may one even ask? . . .when neither of two plays by Racine breaks any of the rules of French drama, is there a permitted basis for finding one of them better than the other?' I was fond of that sort of thing. My mental image of Mason, pale and puffy and slippered in the blue-carpeted room off Jesus Lane, has him squinting through clouds of Balkan Sobranie pipesmoke and unreal beams of sunlight, trying to gauge the length of the awful essay I am reading him, perhaps the particularly long one on Conrad I brought back after vacation.

On the other hand, my mental image of Leavis is unusual (for me) in being a side-view, effectively full profile. I am not sure how much interpretive weight to put on this but it is somehow appropriate. At the end of my first term with him his report to my tutor, who was head of classics in the college and read it to me, had me well placed as 'crippled for life by a classical education'. I am sure he never changed this view and to say even that much is already to make myself too large on the scene. This was a harassed time for Leavis. His wife Queenie was ill. *Scrutiny*, the magazine they had laboured to keep going, was petering out. There were an unusual number of quarrels of an unproductive kind going on with the TLS, BBC and others. He was struggling to finish the crucial book on D. H. Lawrence. Some fatigue may have shown in his teaching, which could fall into repeating old routines – though anyone teaching with the intensity and frequency he sustained is likely to do this on occasion.

Perhaps it should still be stated clearly that 'close reading' was not what was specific to Leavis, though he did it or something like it. What were specific to Leavis, in my experience, were a temperament and a set of stances and a set of values. The stances were something between implicitly principled positions and postures from which one could effectively launch oneself, and they were embodied in certain critical performances by himself and others. The values were established in exemplary pieces of literature, often good sections out of mixed wholes, read in his way. It took me time to adjust to Leavis's unwillingness to describe procedures and criteria in general terms: I would have liked an explicit method with precepts and procédés, and would have given much for the ghostly book 'Authority and Method' he never finished – though the bits of it that emerged later in essays make it clear that this would not have been the sort of neat driver's manual I thought I wanted. Eventually I did see and accept that he could not and need not and should not produce such a thing, but before this I had made my own reduction of some of the going terms into a brief glossary, four closely typed pages, an illegitimate document I

showed no one and shall not expose here, except a short specimen of the texture:

> *Impersonality*
> 'Impersonal': not direct address from the poet;
> self-effacement, disinterestedness, detachment. But
> only in certain circumstances does one talk about
> it (Wordsworth, Keats). See Leavis on 'Hyperion'
> for his treatment. Related to the question of form
> – need for living rhythm not to be stifled by it
> (Lawrence on Mann). Loci: Eliot's 'Tradition and
> the Individual Talent' (reaction against Romantic
> confusion of autobiography and art); Sturge
> Moore for Flaubert tags (who first used the term
> 'impersonality'); Richards Principles pp. 245ff.;
> Coleridge Ch. 15 on 'Venus and Adonis'. A big
> question is whether Lawrence lacked impersonality
> in Women in Love and whether it matters.

It is striking how many of the references, over the whole, are
to French literature.

In my memory the profile-view Leavis, weathered and side-
burned, animatedly projecting his charm, is in a low, battered
armchair in his room, one hand hanging with a book, as if about
to drop it expressively on the floor. He taught us through seminars conducted around cyclostyled reading sheets with anything
from a couple to half-a-dozen text extracts on them; the texts,
verse or prose, were unidentified (though not always unrecog-
nized) and the group attributed them to authors or to moments,
on the basis of legitimate kinds of point drawn from alert reading. This stage was a sort of high connoisseurship. Then Leavis
would expand on a more general issue the texts on the sheet were
calculated to raise: impersonality, movement, or whatever it

might be. At first sight there was little special apparatus to pick
up. Language was treated as transparent through to a social person behaving; or so it seemed. To be curious about the technical
detail of the medium as a medium was to take one's eye off the
ball of Life, as I. A. Richards had done. On the other hand there
was an approved critical literature to know, the basis for a sort of
case law, and there was a structure of implicitly stipulative terms
– fiercely stipulative because they were common words – intel-
ligence, realize, image and many more – used in slightly special
senses, again established by their use in the critical literature.
There were also touches or fragments of something like a vitalist
ideology. In short, one was entering an implicit system.

My rare attempts at contributing to the discussions were always disastrous. I remember remarking that an indication that a
poem on a sheet was by Henry Vaughan was that it had 'Welsh
rhymes'. It was indeed by Vaughan (who happened to be a bearing for me) but my invoking 'Welsh rhymes' exasperated Leavis.
'That is a piece of information I just would not *have*', he gasped.
I had simply meant, as I tried to explain, that some of the rhymes
work in a straighter and so different way when spoken with a
Welsh intonation, as often happens in Vaughan:

> I would (said I) my God would give
> The staidness of these things to man! for these
> To his divine appointments ever cleave,
> And no new business breaks their peace . . .

('These' are birds, bees and flowers.) It is not much of a point
in itself but seems admissible because it leads on to Vaughan's peculiar rational gait. However, Leavis had been cued to a familiar
topic and began a routine on the barrenness of pursuing Gerard
Manley Hopkins's interest in Welsh bardic metres, which some
Oxford literary historian had done – a different kind of point, I

still think. Anyway, I had once more made a classicist's observation – external, information-based and dead.

Leavis was very much a temperament and one key to the temperament was his histrionic energy, his play-acting – much more deeply so than its obviousness might suggest. He marvellously retained and elaborated an almost childish dramatizing impulse long after most people have had it knocked out of them. It appeared in plenty of minor guises, like the exhibitions of athleticism and the intermittent public fasts at high table, but it was basic. I am not placed to have an opinion on how far it was personally self-protective against other strong identities or against a professional situation. It had a part in his performances as outsider and victim of conspiracies and there it may have had destructive effects his collaborators pointed out at the time. But what interested me (or interests me now?) was that role-playing distinguishable from this had such a creative part in his criticism.

Again, one sometimes glimpsed a surface version of it when he read verse aloud. I have never heard poetry as well read as by Leavis on two or three occasions in those seminars. Others have remarked on its force. It was in a general style of expository reading that went back in Cambridge, I now gather, to Mansfield Forbes and I. A. Richards. He often chose to undercut it by guying it or withholding it, but I felt that behind almost all his best criticism there was an extraordinary actor sustaining at once distinct stylized voices for text, author, reader, sometimes also character. (These four may jingle a little with Richards's 'meaning' – sense, feeling, tone, intention – but here it is a matter of voices.) He must himself have habitually *read* like this, I think, sitting silent with a book, voices competing or twining in his mind. It was clearly part of his extreme sensitivity to movement in language. And even when he is simply reporting in his uningratiating critic's voice on the balance he has observed, such reading had come before. It is a pity if that critic's voice – a quite different but also role-playing voice – is taken too exclusively as representing his mind. The mind was among other things a virtuoso reader aloud to itself.

In an odd way the intensity of his moral response to literature seemed driven partly by the same impulse. If you act out text, character, author and reader you are going to find yourself having to inhabit people you will have strong feelings about having had to *be* – 'judgements about life' indeed. And the status of his confidence in his moral judgement could be elusive unless one had a sense of this. Here a person was in an exposed position with Leavis. The famous pattern of exchange – 'This is so, is it not?' 'Yes, but . . .' – involved a reciprocal declaration of identity, tacit in one's own case, of course, but stark and agonistic: it was his humane response or yours. In fact, it was him or you. And since he had a much more realized and coherent critical identity than yourself, it was hard not to find your independent responses casual and shallow, personal blind spots and accidental fads, as of course they often were. A critical crux – an inability genuinely to share his feeling about a text – might be a moment in learning to read but it might be an irreducible difference in that judgement about life. This exposure was exciting.

Reflective excitement in reading is what I remember. This was entirely new to me and due to Leavis. I read great quantities with much energy, though I had less appetite for reading criticism and never went to the libraries to seek recherché items of criticism out: in fact I never developed a mature critical stride at all. What I liked to do was buy a physically compact text – say Kenneth Muir's 'Muses Library' Marvell or the 'World's Classics' Tennyson or the Penguin Hopkins – and live with it for a time, until the pages became limp and docile and I had the illusion of having got it. It was a kind of solemn hedonism, rather like slowly eating good fruit.

I could reconstruct reasons for my being clear at the end of these two or three years with Leavis that, in spite of the value I put on them and on him, literary criticism proper was not the pursuit for me, but it would not be interesting even to myself. It would be a matter of such mixed things as a sense that my range of immediate gut sympathy in literature was too eccentric; and a dislike many of us felt for a type of epigone much in view at that time, dishing out dismissals in the late *Scrutiny*; while at the same time one certainly did not want to abjure. And there was a related nostalgia for the wider scope of the early *Scrutiny* – the 1930s again. Most of all, I just had interests growing in other things.

Reading over this description of Leavis I am struck by a lack of authenticity. It is compromised by the tidiness of something written up in a few pages of epideictic moves, the topics that crop up when a person is being described. This is tolerable since I know that that is so and can take it into account. What is not under control is that, in spite of my taking care with tenses, the language of the description infuses what I feel now into what I felt then, and what I felt then was not static but went through moods and phases and was much less cut-and-dried. And when is 'then', precisely? Properly I should confine myself to now.

I could say: what I directly remember now about Leavis is less secure than what I recognize as Leavis-derived in my own lamination. For instance, I am sure it is due to Leavis that I regularly worry about relevance – about whether some thought about an object, veridical though it may be, is likely to sharpen or just encumber its vitality ('Welsh rhymes'); that I also feel that in art the technical and the moral fuse into one, and that to try and isolate either is likely to be frustrating and may turn destructive; and that there is something meritorious as well as pleasurable about art that arises from trade between the high-cultivated and the demotic (which, by the way, is not the high art/low art duality). Leavis would not have said any of these things in these coarse flat terms, and also I am sure others have said them too, but *I* got these and other such dispositions from him.

Or I could say: I find Leavis hard to read nowadays, particularly what he wrote after my time, whereas I find the William Empson of *Seven Types of Ambiguity* still exhilarating to read. That is partly because the Empson is so sharply focused, while Leavis was trying to keep lots of things in play and many of them belong to a literary-critical politics no longer present. It is also a matter of their critical voices. Both are contrived, and Empson's near-flip terseness is one of the most elegant voices of the time, a poet's invention. I do not think it matters that Leavis's voice lacks this sort of elegance: it is suited to register the complicated balances, allusions and qualifications he wanted to register. My problem with it is a resistance developed in fifty years' struggle not to parrot his tone of voice.

Supposing one had tried to do a Leavis on visual art, on pictures and sculpture and so on, what would it have been like? I was occasionally thinking about this at that time. I cannot isolate much of what I thought about it then precisely because the thinking was integral enough to me for it to metabolize into what I thought later and think now. But certainly the obvious first issue was how one would have to adapt to meet the demands of the different medium. I remembered – and had noted in my epitome – an occasion when Leavis had been disposing of some critic who had invoked the notion of 'beauty' in relation to some poem. Beauty was not a legitimate or helpful term in literary criticism, though, he went on to say without much emphasis, it probably was legitimate when used of visual art. It was not an important matter to him and I am not sure what he had in mind: something like the Golden Section perhaps. Yet it could be taken as a license to mutate.

An overriding difference is that literature registers consciousness of life and the world in the same medium as the critic uses: language. Literary criticism is verbal behaviour all the way, object and subject. There are all sorts of qualifications to be made, about the literary language being distinct from the critical lan-

71

guage and about the difference between language and depiction not being a simple difference between a conventional medium and an analogue medium, but the fact remains that visual art is behaviour in shapes and colours, and – short of dancing or painting it – art criticism's language is in a different relation to visual art. There are many contingent differences too, such as the roles of physical matter and site, and of time, and of intrinsic conditions of the sense. *Scrutiny* had had an active music critic in Wilfred Mellers but no such talent writing on art. It offered no obvious model. While I was at Cambridge I found myself reading Ruskin, not so much *Modern Painters* or *The Stones of Venice* as the compact *Seven Lamps of Architecture* for the confidence with which it locates plain values immanent in art; and Heinrich Wölfflin for the third and last part of *Classic Art* (1899), which seemed to offer some basic critical categories. These, plus (for different reasons) Erwin Panofsky's *Meaning in the Visual Arts*, were what I liked of what I knew, mainly. Roger Fry I respected but did not warm to. What I wanted was a short cut directly between visual properties and social values. There is none, though I should acknowledge that for some years L. C. Knights's *Drama and Society in the Age of Jonson* played an oddly exemplary part in my canon.

(Since writing this I have happened on a dispiriting document, a long, unpublished book review I wrote for a journal planned but not realized by my friend Geoffrey Strickland. The book – Patrick Heron, *The Changing Forms of Art*, mainly a cobbling together of ten years' exhibition reviews in *The New Statesman* – and my review are both of 1955, the year after I came down from Cambridge. I bungle the issue of Heron's confused antithesis between 'abstraction' and 'figuration'. My manner is spuriously knowing and the tone is appalling.)

IV
PERAMBULATION
1955–8

I.

In my last year at Cambridge I had decided, or at least discovered a firm intention, not to commit to a trade or profession for ten years: I was twenty and could have till thirty before settling. Printing was no longer the goal. One ambition I had was to write novels. To find out if I could write novels would take time, not just for writing but for living: I was aware I lacked experience of life, out of which good novels are known to be written. I would keep afloat by teaching or perhaps by entering on some cursus of academic research. My model here may well have been D. J. Enright – later the author of *Memoirs of a Mendicant Professor* – whom I had heard about and admired. The sort of novel I had in mind was not the high novel or avant-garde novel, not the line of Lawrence or of Joyce. What drew me was the possibility of writing good middlebrow fiction. Some of the best Conrad seemed just that, but coming from another category I would have mentioned Eric Ambler and a dozen others working in what would now be called genre fiction. It was well below the level of, say, an Angus Wilson or Iris Murdoch I thought I might try for a niche. The ambition was not realized because I did not have real narrative vitality, but it underlay a zigzag self-direction in the next half-dozen years.

(The first novelist I had known, my Ur-novelist, wrote popular historical novels with – as some recent re-reading reveals

– a distinctively sombre tone and serious material detail. This was the Australian Philip Lindsay – the impressive Jack Lindsay's younger brother – a red-faced, moustached man who due to some kind of wartime pressure found himself briefly teaching at Chepstow towards the end of the war. Previously he had also been in the film business for a time, with Korda. He would wile away English lessons by reading us action scenes from his books, such as *Gentleman Harry Retires* and *Here Comes the King* (squeamish US title *Royal Scandal*, 'the most reckless love in the wickedest court in history'). The colourful dust-jackets with the puffs of his other books on the back and his bohemian dishevelment in general were attractive and I cultivated him, or toadied. I carried up to his room the crates of liquor that came for him by van, and stayed for conversation. I lent him an unreadable book by Cecil Day Lewis given me by my father, called something like *Poetry Ahoy!*, and was content not to get it back. After a term or so he went up to London for a weekend and was never seen at the school again, but in the ten years after the war he was prolific and stayed in view. He is still my default type of a working literary man, partly because his persona was itself almost a cliché from a pre-war popular novel – he might have been written by Eric Linklater – and I am still slightly put out that literary people are, as they always are, different from him.)

After Cambridge I had an untidy exploratory year, in fact, extenuated but not justified by unexpected rejection for the two years' national service of those times. I hadn't fixed myself up with a job. I did a variety of things that year, from house-painting to working on my Italian, but none for very long or to much effect. The basic business of the year was deciding whether literature or visual art should be my longer-term concern and what I should do about it. For a couple of years I had been inclining to the art but a complication was that I did not want to follow in the footsteps of my father, who by this time was director of the Na-

tional Galleries of Scotland. Visual art was his thing and therefore not for me. Adolescence died hard. I remember from this
year certain high moments of decision or revelation. One was
on the railway viaduct at Pontefract, where I suddenly became
clear that I should not take the job I had just been offered after
an interview at a Sheffield grammar school, or any like it. Another was a moment camping in a windless glen on a deer forest
in Wester Ross, where I felt panic fear. And this was the period
when I most got to know Edinburgh, to which my parents had
moved a couple of years before. But the year was incoherent and
does not lend itself to the present purpose. I did however apply
for and got, through the British Council, a modest scholarship to
go to Italy for the next year: the project was to learn about the
Italian Renaissance in its bearing on Renaissance England.

So in the autumn of 1955 I went to Italy. For the winter I would
base myself on the university at Pavia, fifteen miles south of Milan: come spring I would hit the road. Part of my scholarship
was room and board at the Collegio Borromeo at Pavia, an unusual institution. The Collegio had been founded and endowed in
1562 by San Carlo Borromeo to house a score or two of superior
students and, still sustained by the Borromeo family, now had
something like eighty, including half-a-dozen foreigners. It is a
grand mannerist building by Pellegrino Pellegrini tucked away
in a quiet area of the town near the river: an ornate façade addressing a usually empty piazza, a slightly oppressive *cortile* on
two storeys with mezzanine rooms above both, a great frescoed
state *Salone*, and other handsome rooms and a chapel on ground
level; an open eighteenth-century garden behind. It just gets into
Vasari's *Lives* (1568), mentioned as a *palazzo della Sapienza* under
construction. No formal teaching took place there but it was the
site of lectures and conferences, and had a library. I had been ap-
prehensive that being in such a place would be a constraint, but it
turned out well enough.

For one thing the ambience and my immersion in it made quick work of language learning: my basically Dante-derived Italian had to evolve fast there, since one lived – for instance, one ate – in Italian. The conduct of the dining hall, in fact, was one of the things unfamiliar to me. Each of the eighty of us had his prescribed place at tables raised on a dais round four sides of the room, sitting only on the inside side, back to the wall like the Last Supper in a picture, or like some council or consistory. There was no high table. Standing in the middle of the room the frog-like manciple directed with graceful gestures white-gloved and liveried waiters, slim quick men. Conversation was both general – sometimes shouted – and local. At my table were Donagemma, the deeply religious and quite spherical college glutton (the problem of whose geometry during an act of love was pitilessly gone on about at our end of the room); Guardamagna, medicine, a sanguine man interested mainly in football and drink; and Colombo, an ascetic lawyer whose passion was left-wing politics from a Nenni-Socialist position. From him I first learned about the dazzling Gramsci. Other sites of my education were the billiard room and a couple of cheap little bars south of the river in Borgo Ticino where the serious drinking was done.

The Rector of the Collegio Borromeo was Don Cesare Angelini, a tiny man of seventy with a Lombard beak of a nose and pale grey eyes. In the First War he had been a chaplain with the Alpini on the Austrian front, and he had become Rector here just before the Second. He was a local man, proudly a peasant's son but also something of a literary figure, a belletrist and a friend of greater writers. There may have been sad aspects to his isolated life in the place – certainly there was a sharp melancholy in the guitar he would pluck in his garden on summer nights – and people complained of his spying on students and so on. But for myself I liked him and enjoyed conversation with him. I did so quite often. Danes and Germans (he felt and stated) were likely to take to drink whereas the French and Spanish, mature latins, were not (though there were other problems about the French), but the English might go either way: a predecessor from England had been an exhibitionist drunk and I think the reason I was summoned for conversation was to be looked at for symptoms. We both worked hard and for me they were interesting encounters, though I was too stiff to get on easy terms.

Someone who did get on terms with him was the closest of my friends among the other foreigners, the Dane Martin Berg. Martin, in his early thirties, was an achieved novelist and translator. A research project into Lombard Romanesque, for which he was nominally here, was rather a fiction. Mornings he did his own writing. Afternoons now and then he would come with me to the small art history library and leaf with beaming pleasure through the fine illustrations of Kingsley Porter's corpus of Lombard early Romanesque brickwork. More afternoons we went for walks, discussing life or the immediate problems of Martin's books – what had come up that morning. I was struck by how often these were questions about the precision of our memory of common experience. For instance, in hot summer woodlands would a short shower of rain bring out the scents or suppress them for a time? You might say, if the writer does not immediately know, better leave it out; and indeed one soon gets into trouble trying to cogitate it through. But it interested me that the realization of a novel should depend so much on writer's and readers' common unstrained access to organized observation of the everyday: that this should be, so to speak, a medium.

In Pavia I was a little out of alignment with the university. It was still a Renaissance university in the respect that its staple subjects were law and medicine. Literature and art were marginal and each covered by a person who nipped down from Milan just a couple of days a week in term. The literature man, Lanfranco Caretti, was very good indeed. Through the winter his main course was on Tasso's *Gerusalemme liberata*, though he also taught a clever course on the periodical *La Ronda*, 1919–23. Like the only satisfying classics lectures I had heard at Cambridge – R.A.B.Mynors on Lucretius – Caretti on Tasso took the medieval form of commentary-lectures working through a text, a slow and careful reading of the book. It seems to me still the most profitable way to frame a lecture series, if lecture series must be given, and there are real subtleties in sustaining the balance and pitch. Caretti went on to great things in Florence.

As for art, the art man at Pavia was not bad but strange. Wart (or sometimes Edoardo) Arslan was a plump, shy man who at that time was practising a sort of transcendent connoisseurship, attribution to hands become absolute. For the winter semester his lectures were entirely devoted to constructing an oeuvre for the Venetian painter Lazzaro Bastiani. ('About 1430–1512. Pupil of Bartolomeo Vivarini; close follower of Gentile Bellini; influenced by Giovanni Bellini as well and, not improbably in later years, by Carpaccio and Cima': Berenson's Lists.) Some of the troubles with Lazzaro Bastiani are the interminable time span, the grotesque heterogeneity of the people he is supposed to have tried to paint like, a lack of documentation and of conspicuous commissions, really an almost total absence of coherent identity. Excuses could be made for teaching such a topic – 'window on a period'; 'case study: this is how we do it'; 'exhibits a problematic' – but as the same set of thirty bad black-and-white slides turned up week after week in the light of this or that episode of attribution, it all seemed to become unreal. Whether or not Arslan's ascriptions were correct, in the sense of corresponding with events, was simply not an appropriate question: the performance was in some quite other domain.

Don Angelini had warned me I might not find Wart Arslan 'poetic' and I did not. A more lively challenge was the actively poetic character of Don Angelini himself. Here was another culture. His favoured modes were a gentle literary history – mainly around such Lombard writers as Manzoni and Ugo Foscolo – and short virtuoso evocations of landscapes and their moods. It was these latter that intrigued me because, while I would have recoiled from such arch simplicity in English, such careful music and modest display of the right word, here in Italian clearly the coordinates were quite different. Different literary facts were being played off and a different linguistic anatomy was exercising, and I had too insecure a sense of these to be uppish about them in any way. And one learned vocabulary.

I shall give myself the pleasure of trying to translate a page of Angelini. It is from a small collection called *Cinque terre (e una certosa)* – my copy oddly but typically inscribed to me as *borromaico per sempre e letterato per vocazione* – and is about the country east of Pavia, in autumn.

Few lands give such sense of richness, of sheer fatness, as the plain of Lodi, desirable land, distinguished land, land shot through by streaks of sun and by a water that has been coaxed with benign cunning to run between field and field: ornament and nourishment, quickness and life. Or, that water is channelled into gutters or ditches or gullies that accompany the roads for quite long stretches, two on the one side of the road and two on the other, giving and gaining a robust majesty. A genial system of irrigation and cultivation this, on which still shines the ancient Benedictine wisdom that first thought it and ordained it.

And it is due precisely to this bountiful presence of water, its support of exuberant growth, that it is easier to find here the signs and images of a magical autumn. For, with its slow and exquisite unmantling, autumn is most sensible and solemn where the opulence of growth during the rich and easy seasons has been greatest; and among the richest we know no other like that of this fertile and

milk-yielding land, stridden through by unending rows
of poplars and of willows, of elders and of planes, and its
vast meadows loud with bellowing huddles of kine, grazed
by beasts that, out in the middle of those fields, have the
solemnity of monuments.

Autumn, I was saying, is more sensible here through
the human-like self-divestment of our familiars the trees,
which, if in spring and summer they created quintains and
stage sets for imaginary dramas, and on this stage seemed
themselves to belong to both audience and company of
players, now register spaces, solitudes, silences; and the
land expands to match the span of the sky. Truly autumn
here finds its exaltation, consuming all form; what might
seem likely to make the countryside poorer and less fine
really enriches it with a contemplative virtue and the
melancholy that comes when beauty has been fulfilled.

All this is as if to say: spring may give this land a
body, but autumn gives it a soul. And he who seeks the
spirit residing in the Lodi country does well to be there
in autumn, when it is transfigured by assumption of the
visible form into invisible form. The waters, so abundant
– 'watery Lombardy'! – run more lively and clean in the
ditches then; in the meadows an exhausted greenness is
fading away like the notes of a flute faltering in the wind;
and the wetness proper to the season prompts the forming
of mists, dreamlike mists that endow this land with that
reticent glamour of modesty, a veil with which it is covered
even while in the act of making itself bare.

Blessed ambiguity of autumn!

Any resemblance to Lush Places is my fault. It goes on to
colours, colours of the leaves in their final agony and of complex
sunsets.

1. *With Renate*
2. *On the farm, in Radnorshire*

3. *In Snowdonia*
4. *At Manchester Grammar School (back row, third from left)*

5. At Cambridge
(middle row, second
from left)
6. Munich library card

7. *In Copenhagen with Martin Berg and an unidentified friend*

8. *At the Victoria & Albert Museum*

That year the Lombard autumn soon gave way to winter, in fact, a period of snow and ice and a coarser fog. Pavia, a town of brick and towers, at that time physically shabbier and less explicit than nowadays, was mysterious, perhaps even poetic, in this fog. My room, high-ceilinged and big-windowed and tile-floored, was cold. I read there in bed under all possible covers and ate cheap cooking chocolate to satisfy a craving for sugar.

I took to going to Milan. Pavia is a satellite of Milan, and Milan is still the Italian city I have most personal feeling for, though I have since spent more time in several others. I caught the bus into Milan for the museums and bookshops, for the Piccolo Teatro (Goldoni and Pirandello, Visconti and Strehler) and to see a girl I had met on the Calais/Basel train to Milan coming out, but the place took a general hold. I cannot understand a preference for, say, Florence – as a city. My images of Milan are in bright morning or in a dusk of early evening, lamps just lit but the sky still participating; I do not recall the frequently oppressive Lombard afternoons. I am not sure how interesting the question of one's retrospective sense of cities really is, the question of what causes our remembering a particular city with fondness or not. Beyond the objective virtues of a place, and how good or bad one's actual experiences there have been, much of it seems associational or allusive: Milan had a strong and very particular nineteenth-century atmosphere that I found and find romantic. But I know I have a liking for a type of city – Lisbon, Munich, Edinburgh, Milan . . . – in which certain real characteristics recur: big but not quite first-rank in scale; a particular balance of diversity and order in its layout; some dominant bipolarity or dialectic in its historical character; noticeable light; and, I think, an energetic and justified self-absorption in its people. No tail-wagging.

In March I began travelling, trips of a week or two between which I would return to Pavia for a few days to refit and read up a little for the next. My first outing was to Venice (city of Lazzaro Bastiani) but later trips were often to lesser centres and most days in the Veneto or the Marches or Lombardy I moved on. I lived frugally – lunch in a dairy, often, and perhaps a room in a widow's house learned of at the bus station. Small-town bus stations were a social amenity and I found the world of dusty blue buses going to remote small places very romantic indeed. On the whole evenings were solitary and spent on my notes, maps and timetables, and presumably some sort of aesthetic digestion. I now find these trips mysterious and yet I am also sure they were foundational for me. I had travelled in Italy before – a long-vacation trip with two Cambridge friends in a landrover – but not in this way. I now quartered regions and combed cities with lists of what I wanted to see. The lists I had adapted mainly from Raimond Van Marle's questionable but well-illustrated *Development of the Italian Schools of Painting* (1923–38). When I found the piece I wanted I just looked at it and waited for enlightenment. Or rather I attended on my own response. It seems to me strange now that I should have had such confidence in sustained direct address to so much art. I had practically no knowledge or information about it, since I had read so little. I must have flagged sometimes and the notes of observations from this period I occasionally come upon are pale and useless.

But these encounters either set or met problems that engaged me for years after. Did one need to think, to conceptualise about the character of these objects in order to get a grasp of them? Probably, but with what concepts? Their concepts? Was knowledge of the historical frame – art history but also cultural history – properly to be sought as a condition of understanding? Surely: their strangeness was hair-raising and insisted on questions about their circumstances. What then was the standing of the raw visual *feel* of the pictures and the immediate sense of human quality and mood? And could one evaluate the objects, relatively? One was doing so anyway; but then what was one's status?

The main critical conviction I had developed independently at Cambridge was the very general one that it was no use denying or excluding elements in your response to a work, as inappropriate or improper. If there was a strong element of sentimentality in your response, or a degraded romanticism, or susceptibility to some kitschy charm of tone, it did not help to try banishing such parts of oneself. They were intrinsic to one's energy. They probably would not be suppressed anyway. The thing to do was to identify the impulses, perhaps try to chasten them a little and ride their energy and in some cases perhaps discount them, but above all simply to know them for what they are. I wouldn't have said this in quite these terms then but I would have produced something like the last half-dozen lines if challenged on that ground. It was part of a general attitude I referred to, to myself, as 'selective drifting' – a grand but also ironic principle that was partly about directing effort where it would have effect but partly also an evasion of issues of free will and determinism.

This was the first year I had spent outside of Britain and one thing I began working through was a relation to nationality. Perhaps 'work through' puts it too kindly since it was hardly a campaign of constructive reflection, more a long sequence of petty episodes of feeling, discrete and miscellaneous – arguments with Colombo about the Cyprus troubles, recognition of priggish elements in one's sexual self, nostalgia for absent snugness (on the infantile level of winter tea-times and toasting forks), sightings of horrific British tourists and the dreadful Italian rich, intimations of the thinness of British painting and also of post-Renaissance Italian verse, and worries about the lot of some cats and dogs and poor people in Italy. . . . It would be tedious to prolong this: I simply want to register the mix and the low level. The process of coming to terms with such local cultural realities is perpetual, an accumulation of experience and adjustment and shifting balances, but it happened that the only two real encounters I had with Britishness that year were discouraging.

In Rome for a month I stayed in the relative comfort of the British School in the Borghese gardens. It was the economical thing to do and the room I had was good for reading and writing in, but the place was humanly hard work. It is surprising no one wrote a murder story of the Agatha Christie kind about the British School of that time since the components of one kind of such stories were there – a detached group of diversified middle-class Britons leading a quite anachronistic formalized life against the exotic background of the city, into which some of the Brits sometimes went. I drop no names but there were, I reckoned, three urgently eligible victims and two others who would not be missed. I arrived in early spring and people had been at close winter quarters for several months. As an uncommitted unit I was assailed with confidences and versions, but I was a passive listener because, though of course I had not forgotten my English, somehow it was not on the tip of my tongue just then. I thought English thoughts in English but could not very spontaneously speak them, being linguistically stiff by constitution and the winter of immersion in Italian having had this effect.

It occurs to me now, though it did not at the time, that as a building the School was a metaphor of a kind of Englishness I deplored but found stubbornly present in myself. If one is prepared to be humourless about it, the structure is a fraud on just too many levels. All façade, it descends from the British pavilion built on the same site for the Rome international exposition of 1911. Edwin Lutyens had been architect of that and became architect of this. It is somewhere between the pastiche it purports to be and straight kitsch – (1) Palladian enough to feel wrong in Rome but (2) a thoroughly sanitized, British Palladianism in which (3) sly Ned is as usual asserting his own presence too noisily, this time with his nasty grandiose lateral spread of the elements of the facade, a tiresome trick soon to mark late-imperial New Delhi. There is – or was: the interior has since been rebuilt – no architecture behind the facade, just a hollow square of snug nondescript rooms.

The British School was not part of my England. I had known none of the people previously. The only English acquaintance I remember re-encountering that year in Italy was a man called Morris Shapira, who I ran into in Florence. I confined the Cambridge pages here to a sketch of the figure of Leavis, as most to my purpose. There seem quite enough memoirs of the Cambridge of the period and mine would just be a lower-profile and immaturer person's variant. Morris Shapira, who appears in various of the memoirs and at least one of the novels, had been a year or so ahead of me at Cambridge and would in a few years be Leavis's assistant and designated successor at Downing for a time, though things turned out badly for him and ended in disaster. He was not exactly a friend of mine and indeed had been away at Harvard for much of my period, but he was a friend of the epically decent Stendhal scholar Geoffrey Strickland, as was I: I remember once feeling shabby when Geoffrey loyally chided me for making a joke about the absent Morris, whom actually I found intimidating as well as comic. This time in Florence, encountered near the Uffizi, he set me, as Italian interpreter, to finding him somewhere to stay and this led to our trudging what seemed most of the most charmless streets of north central Florence looking at places. The trouble was simply that he wanted somewhere better and above all – as he spelled out to me – cleaner, visibly cleaner, than he would pay for. I no longer recall what we got for him.

What I recall is his sheer presence on the hot, pale, dusty sidewalks. It was one of the periods when progressive people were wearing black leather – though I am not sure how far the practice was current and coded in Italy itself then – and Morris, perhaps cued by the poet Thom Gunn, had gone into leather whole-hog. In black biker's boots, and lustrous in black leather breeches and black leather jacket, carrying an admittedly plastic helmet that vouched for an actual, probably very large machine not far away and so legitimized the gear, he was a figure to see. He held himself well. Physiognomically – dark, pale, fine-featured and already balding – he could easily have been a Florentine, even the object of a Bronzino portrait, but his majestic manner of moving along streets had a grandeur that was not the Italian grandeur because it was not directed to a beholder. People stared all right, but his *figura* existed for himself, the strut of some real confidence even if also urged by leather breeches. Shambling along next to him, I thought – as he must have prompted many to think – what poor hams the two motor-cyclist death riders in Cocteau's *Orphée* had been: Morris here *was* menace. During the couple of days we coincided in Florence I found his self-assurance a threat and this reminder of Cambridge ridiculous.

Offputting updates from England, then. I never resolved the nationality problem, though over the years it lost urgency at the same time as it became more complex. A showy alienation from many things British I was professing by the end of this Italian year was felt, but callow.

That was 1955–6. There are many Italies, by which I refer not to the many and very different regions but to one's take on a particular place on different particular occasions. The places are layered, iridescent with varied sets and coteries and institutions. Within the next dozen years I would revisit many of the same towns with rather different focus and accreditation, seeking out humanist manuscripts in small reading-rooms and at one stage spending time in a still rather Aldous Huxley-ish expatriate Tuscan ambience. But the dusty blue-bus northern Italy of 1956 remained the base.

2.

1956–7 I spent in St Gallen in north-east Switzerland. Half way through the previous year in Italy I had realized that for me – novelist or not – art would be a thing to study, but for that I should need money. I also felt I should need German. It seemed rational to invest a year in acquiring both by teaching in Switzerland, so I got the *Times Educational Supplement* and fixed myself up.

The Institut auf dem Rosenberg was up on a ridge on the outskirts of the town: an international school with three or four hundred pupils and sixty teachers, expensive but not select, the buildings of a pre-1914 Teutonic chalet character. The language of the school outside classes was German, except on Sundays. I taught English in the Swiss, Italian and German sections and a little Latin in the 'Anglo-American' (or miscellaneous) section, and had my share of general supervision. My purpose was to earn money and learn some German in preparation for studying in Germany.

My sense of this year, offhand, is unfocussed and almost without events but quite strong in atmosphere, even if it is difficult to be explicit about what the atmosphere was. I suspect much of it was generated by my reading: this was a year when I was reading German novels. But I do have a thin folder of odds and ends from that time – school list and rule-book and such, map, a few photographs, no letters – and I shall try to use this to prime memory.

As a first cue, documentation of regular activity in the folder is distorted by the anxieties of a man called Reinhard. To catch the tone:

> After lunch and after tea the Seniors' supervising-masters make a control through their houses (unpermitted smoking, unpermitted visits to other boys' rooms, fighting in the rooms, etc.). With this control they combine a 'control of presence', (*Anwesenheitskontrolle*) for which

they must have a rectified *House-List*. These lists are set up every week and must be got from the *Tagchef* in good time on supervision days. Rounds in the surroundings of the school, at the Schlösslitreppe and the Grünbergtreppe, and now and then in the Restaurant Schoren – in this case the school pays for any drink or so – must be made, after consultation with the *Tagchef*, sporadically. (from Short Instructions for Supervision: English version.)

Nobody did all this sort of thing. Reinhard, an aging man with a big white head like a Hollywood senator, ran the school for someone called Gademann who owned other schools in French Switzerland and rarely appeared. (I have at this moment an 'image' of Gademann arriving in a large American car smoking a cigar, but it is suspiciously like something out of George Grosz.) Reinhard wrote rule-books. We were clear that one main purpose of the rule-books was to cover him and the school when things went wrong. Boys might abscond, or set fires which the complexity of the rules for fires made sure would not be put out, or they might just die in any of three itemized ways in the River Sitter below the school: the rule-books would show in detail that the Direction had foreseen every danger and told someone to stop it. ('Any boy possessing fire-arms or ammunition must deposit them immediately (Nussbaum, Room No. 60)'). But I think the flood of paper from Reinhard was partly also an expression of actual alienation from reality. He was no longer in control of his nerves and sat dictating a universe he could bear the thought of. He could not bear the thought of individual persons, with whom one saw him sink into a twitching, stuttering incoherence. So he wrote a generalised school – not an 'ideal' school but a school without particular human entities.

The teaching, long hours and small classes, was tolerable but the supervision, or *Aufsicht*, was not. My *Aufsicht* was usually in Ulrichshof, fifty thirteen- to fourteen-year-olds, living two or three to a room. Every five days one had a day of *Aufsicht* and it lasted sixteen hours. One woke them at 6.45 for early gym. (The fug in the rooms as one went in to roust them out is securely unforgettable: I see now from the rule-book that they had to shower once a week and in winter were fined 25 Rappen for an open window.) The day finished at 22.30, an hour after lights-out. Twice a term one had a full weekend on, Saturday and Sunday together – a bad weekend. It was not that discipline was particularly difficult: most of the boys were pleasant enough and the fact that many of them were sophisticated for their age made them easier to deal with. The minority of vicious or disturbed boys one learned to squash or, if they were unsquashable, ignore. The trouble lay in the texture of one's time. Pink memo (translated):

Baxandall/Heuberger/Resch/Gärtner/Moser/Härtel
Re: Ulrichshof-Supervision
During big break [10.10–10.25] the Ulrichshof supervising-teacher supervises distribution of the 'snack' in the anteroom of the dining-hall. There he ensures order and calm but also glances occasionally into the two corridors by the ping-pong tables and outside the staff-room where there is frequently shouting and wrangling. Once the first rush of distribution of the 'snack' is past, he makes a quick visit to the upper floors of Ulrichshof and with a glance into every other room assures himself that there also all is in order.
R.
4 June 1957/Wednesday

I was known in Ulrichshof as *Der Tod*.
I am getting little imagery from all this. I cannot raise an image of any of the rooms I rented, the classrooms I taught in, or

of Ulrichshof, except that its floors were pale grey. The interior I remember best in St Gallen is that of the Café Seeger down in the town , the booths alternating blue and buff corduroy and so rationally arranged in the big front and back rooms (these quite different from each other in mood) that I could draw a ground-plan still. I spent half my evenings here, reading, playing chess, meeting friends – nearly all of these being colleagues from the school since we made little contact with the natives. Of the streets and buildings and Abbey of St Gallen I have a tourist's and per-haps a limited shopper's memory, but there are images of one or two particular places, such as the nursery slopes on the other side of town, where I went to begin skiing away from the eyes of the school and found surfaces awkwardly icy from much use. Yet looking now at photographs of the town I can identify and place many of them. There seems a mental map or specification on which I can place but from which I cannot develop images.

The landscape of the region was fine sub-alpine pastoral – rolling meadows and woods with occasional compact gorges. To the north it ran down to the snugly mysterious Lake Constance and to the east there were the pale-brown peaks of the Säntis, the main mountain massif of north-east Switzerland. It was a good ambience for someone reading German novels, classic Roman-tic country for Wilhelm Meister and Josef Knecht to wander in, tidy and cheerful. But though I can visualize and could draw a synthetic impression of it with its typical components, there is no single actual view that I can summon up.

There were people, of course, and many of them interesting and congenial. Again a distinction here: looking at the staff list, I put faces to less than a quarter of the names; but looking at a cou-ple of photographs of Big Break in the staff-room I put names to three quarters of the faces. . . . The multi-purpose Herr Lorenz, the only person I have heard say '*Donnerwetter!*' in anger: mar-ried to dire *Madame* Lorenz, not shown. The wilfully sinister

Professor Zillich, freelance theologian, whose role in the school I never made out: perhaps house casuist. The self-effacing but charming little Dr. Baxa, mathematician, who should not have ended up here. . . . Much acquaintance with mainly pleasant people, easy come but easy go.

One product of trying to prime visual memory of the everyday has been to recall, instead, forgotten petty events – deviations from the everyday. It occurs to me now that I quite often made trips, to Winterthur for pictures, Zurich for books, to Lugano with a friend for privacy, and since I worked in all four Sections there were varied Section binges: the Anglo-Americans tended to have sulky fondue dinners in the town, but the Italians fêted their visiting examiners with a wine-tasting trip round Lake Constance in a bus. I also remember a number of moments from a disorderly two-day excursion up the Flumsberg in Glarus, twenty boys and two teachers.

> Every group-leader should set a *reasonable* Tempo. It is senseless to want to climb a mountain in fast Tempo. More important that pupils learn to walk *calmly* and *steadily* and enjoy landscape beauties as they go. (from Instructions for Leading Excursions, §.8.)

A vivid image has myself and group-leader Dr. Klein, an ironist from Silesia with very pinched features even at good times, staggering down an endless airless path in thick trees: no landscape at all. My own legs are tired from the downhill jolting but Klein is in a really bad way, seriously hung over from too much schnapps the night before in the hut. The boys had had the moral courage to tell him it was too much, which was more than I had done. They are now all gone ahead, far ahead, to get to the station bar in good time before the train. We hope they will only drink beer.

Another isolated vignette, one of the very few images that have recurred to me occasionally in the mean time, is of an Appenzeller peasant wearing the local dress of embroidered black jacket and breeches, barefoot, gold earring. He is quite beside himself with anger and we – this time mild Dr. Bächli from Basel and I on another excursion – are being bawled out in dialect because of our group treading his meadow. ('§.11. Meadows should not be trodden'.) There is something postcard-like about this vignette and I suspect it has been looked at too often.

To return to people, I had relation particularly with four that year, of whom I will try one whom I have not seen since – faintly visible in the far background of one photograph. Andrew, a thin, fair, balding man in his middle thirties, had been at the school for years. He was English but had taken his doctorate at the University of Basel, his thesis being on some sort of nordic philology, and he had good German. He rented a neat modern house about three miles north along the ridge and in the spring suggested I share it: I had met his mother, who was leaving after a long stay, and she had approved. At the time I was living down in the town in a room above a workshop that made fake peasant-baroque furniture, a picturesque Tales of Hofmann-like location – I get an image of the street façade outside but not of the room – where I was becoming depressed by ingrained dirt. With the days drawing out it seemed a good idea to move up the ridge.

In some ways it worked but Andrew was in a difficult patch. He had a long-standing woman-friend in another Swiss town with whom he occasionally communicated and of whom I was now and then shown the same photograph, but he seemed to me too interested in an appalling boy at the school, Jünger. Jünger was fourteen or fifteen, vain, stupid, brushed his hair like Herbert von Karajan, had sly hazel eyes and a pretty flushed tan complexion, and was playing Andrew along. I taught Jünger, which Andrew did not, and I was open about thinking him an all-round pain. I got tired of Andrew gurgling: 'He's a stinker, but I *like* his stink.' And I had not realised how heavily Andrew was drinking. He did much of it at the smart bar of the Hotel Hecht, not to my taste. He would arrive back at the end of a session there, not drunk, well able to ride his moped up the hill, but talkative, and first I had to hear a report of the views on this and that of Horst, the Hecht barman. Horst was a reflective barman, full of tips on that bracer called Life, and during this time Andrew would also be moving irritatingly about, touching things.

Then, after five minutes or so of Horst, he would go over to sit on an upright chair next to his index cabinet. This cabinet was a splendid object, matt pale-grey metal with many small drawers to fit his word-slips, or vice versa, and I remember the slips as being rather larger and squarer than our three-by-five cards. They carried the words and references of his philological research, in principle still a going concern. The drawers were beautifully contrived to coast very smoothly in and out on some first-class arrangement of ball-bearings. Andrew would put one arm not around, but along the top of the cabinet and with his other hand very gently open and shut drawers, tilting his head to hear better. One sometimes sees musicians doing rather the same as they play a stringed instrument. And he would now occasionally make more isolated remarks about whatever was on his mind. It might just be a problem in the Anglo-American section – there were real problems, which I have long forgotten – but more and more it was his sense of being taken advantage of by the Direction of the Institut, particularly Reinhard and Gademann. I cannot remember anything at all of the detail of this either but I know I felt he was right and presumably I said so.

Then, I think near the start of the summer term, Andrew was approached by a known boarding-school in Germany, a cognate of Salem and certainly a much better school than the Institut. It was a straight offer but without the seniority and privileges he had built up at St Gallen. This became the issue. I pressed him to go. I do not know how much weight this had, but all of what purchase I had I used in that sense. He left St Gallen that summer and moved north. I have no idea how things went with him there.

I have long been ashamed of this episode. Even at this moment of writing it up it provokes a physical unease. I had not thought the issue through as fully as I should: how well would a vulnerable man like Andrew bear up in a more testing ambience, less accustomed and accommodating to his oddities? I did not really look beyond my sense that he was heading for a mess in St Gallen. I would still guess he was doing so but that is not the point. Also it was my view that a fresh start for Andrew would be good absolutely: fresh starts in general I favoured at that time. Exasperation with him played too big a part in what I said and so did my own disapproval of the Institut. It adds up to a sort of bad faith, I am afraid. Clearly I had invaded another as one has no business to do.

That summer term I was teaching special early classes at 7.15 and regularly cycled south along the ridge at an early hour. (I see from a bicycle licence in my folder that my machine was a 'Mont Blanc' and the licence is dated April 24, 1957, so that fixes the month I moved in with Andrew. In late July I was going to leave St Gallen to join Martin Berg in Copenhagen, the person who first rang the alarm for me about my improper invasion of Andrew; and some time in late August I went on from Copenhagen by cargo boat to Leith, a voyage unbelievably of two days and three nights allowing much time to think about it all, though I do not remember how much I actually did so; whereas I do remember reading *Felix Krull* and *Point Counter Point* in my bunk.) On the early-morning bicycle rides, more often than not, I saw some sort of sunrise over Austria to the east. Sometimes it was so spectacular I stopped to gaze, even if it meant missing early-class-breakfast at 6.45. One could hardly have an iterative epiphany, but those sunrises accumulated over the three months into some composite my mind used as an open emblem for a number of good things, including fresh starts. I know one could not have a more worn symbol: Sunrise! I think what still sustains its energy for me is the sense of momentary solitude before an overpopulated day.

In spite of the attack on Andrew I feel fairly at ease about the person who negotiated my year in St Gallen but I do not see how he fits in with the rest. It is another lost world, no longer there for verification. Six or seven years later I had brief business about sculpture at the Abbey and was in the town for the inside of a day. I drove up the ridge to the school, principally in the hope of getting the address of a friend, a liberal South African exile who had continued to work for Gademann schools after I left; he had worryingly disappeared a year or so before into what immediately became Wilenski and Smith's Rhodesia. The new head of the Anglo-American section – a bustling, nervous Englishman in an over-gentlemanly tweed suit – was off-hand and denied knowledge of every person's name I offered, including his recent predecessor as head of the section. He made it clear that he wanted nothing to do with riff-raff of my period, standards as well as personnel having altogether changed. My period, I remember this ambitious usher as being explicit, was forgotten. Good day.

3.

1957–8 was in Munich. Many discerning people dislike Munich. I will just declare that there were constants there – the white subalpine light, the gamut of light brown and middle brown colours presented by the buildings, the penetration of the urban by rusticity of varied kinds – that gave me at the time a sense of well-being. Its population reached a million only in the year I was there, but more important than size, it had not then developed its later grossness: fattypuff times were clearly coming but this was still a fairly austere pre-prosperity. There were also many details – snow falling by lamplight on tramlines around the Maximilianeum, the dimly lit Max-Platz at night, the Monopteros in rain – which by association with episodes took on reflected colour. The mechanics of some of it were rather Wordsworthian, but not the coding. I spent time in Munich in later years and liked it less.

That year I lodged comfortably near the Herkomerplatz in Bogenhausen, with an easy walk across the Englischer Garten to the University. The choice had been for location rather than style and my room was in a vast warren-like apartment in multiple occupation. The human atmosphere was more Wedekind than Thomas Mann. In a small room down the corridor one way there was a sweet but simple-minded young street-sweeper, sent off immaculate in his blue uniform each day by an aspiring and very competent wife who acted as general housekeeper – Pomeranian refugees, I think. Every now and then she allowed him to get drunk, when he became puzzled and truculent. In a group of three bigger rooms down the other way there was a middle-aged ménage which I never got quite straight, partly because it was always in flux. The husband shifted between suffering and being liable to suffer from some debilitating condition and stayed in bed a great deal. How far he was simply complaisant and how far the other interest of his wife, a gaunt but lively blond woman, had some cash basis, and if so how urgently necessary this was, was not clear. The other man, a flushed fleshy figure, was irregularly in funds – sharp suit and *Sekt* for all on one day, seedy dressing-gown and moping the next several. None of these three, also from the east, ever seemed to leave the house. There were two or three other people in other rooms.

But I was usually out. I ate out, spent my days in libraries, bookshops and museums, at lectures and just going about. St Gallen had not catered for the flâneur and I was catching up, and music and theatre were so accessible here I could go to something two nights out of three when I wanted. For the first couple of months that was exactly what I wanted and I went around in a state of permanent critical alertness, keenly addressing everything I saw for issues of aesthetico-moral principle. To see even a bad Munich production of *Look Back in Anger*, played as if it was a Viennese farce, was to think about the moral systematicity of genre. Or a more complex case: I saw a certain actor do a totally ham traditionalist Faust at the big Staatstheater, all Aryan profile and monotone chaunting, much applauded; and I then saw him, a month later in a small workshop theatre, give a shattering performance in the comparatively small part of the Actor in Gorky's *From the Lower Depths*, in exactly the same manner, posturing and intoning quite unchanged. What did that say about 'style'?

Or, the omnipresent composer Carl Orff raised questions about the political gearing of art. What had happened to Orff between the 'neo-neanderthal' (Stravinsky's term) works of the 1930s and the simply arid stuff he was bringing out now? What was being cleansed of what, and how, and was it really clean? The key work for these questions, I decided, was *Die Kluge* of 1943 and the answers were depressing. . . . I am indulging for a moment in this much mystification to catch a mood. How to find a stance towards survivals from 1933–45 was a necessary preoccupation and the pressing problem was compromised persons – Orff, or Hans Sedlmayr.

Hans Sedlmayr was Ordinarius in Art History at the University. I had not come to study with him, I had come to Munich for Munich, but I had known he was there and part of what I would be meeting. He was an Austrian of sixty or so who had succeeded Julius von Schlosser in the historic chair at Vienna in 1936 and then been removed from it in 1946. I was told at Munich that Sedlmayr had already been a Party member in the early 'thirties. But then I was also told that his personal affiliations in the middle 'thirties were rather with social-democrats and that he had been caught wrong-footed in 1938 by the *Anschluss*: the *bêtises* (such as a notorious *Heil Hitler!* in a 1938 *Festschrift*) would then be opportunist overcompensation. Both may be true. The facts as to membership seem to be that he joined the Party as early as 1930, left it after a couple of years on the grounds of its unacceptable policy on art, and then rejoined in 1938. In the years after the war he certainly became dependent, for patronage but also for an intellectual niche, on conservative religious circles of a slippery kind, represented by the periodical *Wort und Wahrheit*; and he produced two prominent books of this colour, *Loss of the Centre* (1948), which is an organicist study of various symptomatic kinds of estrangement in art since the industrial revolution, and *The Emergence of the Cathedral* (1950). His appointment in 1951 to the Munich chair, also a historically prominent chair, had been controversial and is still difficult to understand. It was said he had been 'put in by the Dominicans', whatever that meant.

All this I soon learned. What I knew of Sedlmayr when I arrived was *Loss of the Centre* and some hearsay about a method known as 'structure-analysis'. I was interviewed by him about admission to the department and its library, and he did not hide an anglophobia and amusement at my lack of training. I took both these amiss, which was probably stupid. (The anglophobia may have derived partly from the hard time Sedlmayr (I now know) had had in Palestine and the Ottoman territories in 1917–18: I would like to think of him as on the fringes of John Buchan's *Greenmantle*.) He was impressive, with an axe-head-like head and flickering pale eyes, and some sort of fine tremor with which, I came to know, he could bring a fine throb into his voice when lecturing on late Michelangelo and such. On the basis of my having a Bavarian state studentship I was indulged with entry to the 'Exercises for Advanced Students', the *Oberseminar*, as well as the department library. I went to the *Oberseminar* but never warmed to the department or its library, where I sensed an atmosphere of ambitious manoeuvring among students – though by taking one's occasional turn sitting at the library supervisor's desk for late opening one conveniently got to know the people. There were not many more than a hundred registered students at that time.

There was an alternative library, the Central Institute for Art History in the Königsplatz, and after a time I based myself there instead, like other students not at ease with Sedlmayr. The Director of the Zentralinstitut, Ludwig Heydenreich, was an Italian Renaissance scholar I admired and he would be giving a course on Urbino within the university framework in the summer semester; I decided I would write for him rather than for Sedlmayr the paper I felt I ought to produce that year. The walk through the district between the Institute and the University – Alte Pinakothek, Technische Hochschule, small bookshops and antiquaries, a dance school where at one point I had occasion to go for lessons (feeling like the Steppenwolf in Herman Hesse's novel), my travel agent, a couple of favourite cafés – became a cheerful part of routine.

Meanwhile I went to lectures in the Ludwigstrasse and intermittently addressed the issue of Sedlmayr. Most of the other art historians teaching at the university were fairly lacklustre, the independent younger talents like Willibald Sauerländer having been driven out by Sedlmayr, and I see from my *studienbuch* I enrolled for courses with various people I did not persist with and remember little about: instead I went mainly to lectures in other fields, literature and history, the elusive Ernesto Grassi (Dante) and Ernst Schnabel (strong on *Manchestertum*) for instance. Sedlmayr's own full-dress lectures – that year successively on mannerism and on early medieval art – were polished performances for a large general audience: an image has him picking his way with a modest smile through the people sitting in the stepped gangway of a large packed lecture-hall. But the restricted *Oberseminar* was more interesting, and done with some formality.

Normally a student gave a paper on a subject in the area of the last semester's lectures and this was then discussed: Sedlmayr sat alone in the front row of the small lecture-room and three assistants sat behind him in the second row; the two of these assistants who intervened most were Erich Hubala and Mohammed Rassem. At least one assistant had prepared and was checking facts and detail of the case, while Sedlmayr's part was more to comment and enlarge on method. Unlike Leavis he had provided a driver's manual, a couple of mimeographed booklets, the first being in the form of methodical precepts, the second a paradigm analysis of a picture, Bruegel's *Blind Leading the Blind*. These were a basis for expansion here and application to the particular case, a favoured formula for the logic of the process, though not necessarily the order of performance, being:

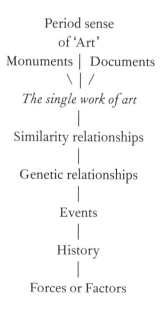

Period sense
of 'Art'
Monuments | Documents
\ | /
The single work of art
|
Similarity relationships
|
Genetic relationships
|
Events
|
History
|
Forces or Factors

Sedlmayr drew this diagram on the blackboard and soon also published it. He evidently saw his own contribution as lying particularly in pre-war development at the second stage, the 'structure-analysis' of the single work. His post-war books moved rather directly between the work of art and the Forces or Factors.

It is still not clear to me how far schemes like this and the structure-analysis format were meant as genuinely theoretical constructions and how far they were just pedagogical drills or routines. Very little in all the procédé and apparatus was actually argued: the premises were aphoristic or arbitrary, for all the systematic presentation. But in the first instance *Struktur* referred to the form of a historical actor's view and construction of the world – how, structurally, he took things. In a second instance it referred to the form in which this offered itself to our experience in a work of art. This idea claimed some theoretical bearings in the earlier Viennese art historian Alois Riegl though more generally there were roots in romantic idealism. The *Struktur* was then actually pursued in the work of art through a multi-level analysis of literal meaning (the matter of representation), allegorical meaning (the cultural codes and symbolisms) and spiritual meaning (visual qualities whose meaning was not coded by culture or period but timeless). These last were sometimes elaborated rather on the model of late-medieval allegory theory.

For me the stumbling block presented itself almost as one of language – simply of the words used in connection or linkage between a visual character and a historical Force or Factor. Behind this, certainly, there would be the more metaphysical issue of how first-instance *Struktur* could relate to second-instance *Struktur*, but I never really got around to that. One got diverted by preliminary troubles in the status of the Forces or Factors. For instance, a slightly comic crux for me here was an odd element in his long book on the cathedral, *Die Entstehung der Kathedrale*.

The gothic cathedral, he proposes, is among other things a synthesis of three principles: the nordic, the romanic and the celtic. His basis for these categories is not clearly established, but linguistic collateral plays a part. Nordic properties were constructiveness and system, tension and verticality. Romanic properties were a warm-sensuous plasticity and rounded fullness associated with the human body and a general moderating humanity. It was the celtic that struck me most. (How did he know me so well?) Celtic properties were: fantasy, *cold*-sensuous colour and glitter, an absence of a sense of boundaries or limits. Courtly love and scholasticism were type celtic cultural creations: also celtic were an incapacity for the tragic or heroic, and lack of a sense of hell. In language the celtic principle, with its pre-indogermanic basis, showed itself in French sentences tripping evenly along and lacking the energy of the structured Latin period or the measured rhythm of the Germanic sentence. In the specific case of the cathedral, celtic contributions were the grotesque, the stained glass and other light effects, and such un-plastic decoration as scroll ornament and general linear interweaving.

There was a deep off-colour silliness about this sort of thing that had the effect of compromising the neat analytical tool box of the Oberseminar. But I repeat that the key problem for me was in the means of connection between the Factor and the visual characteristic, which seemed to me word-play: punning or sometimes metaphor. Sedlmayr did not seem aware of this; if he was aware, certainly he was not in control of it. For instance, in *Loss of the Centre* – which in 1955 had been supplemented by The Revolution of Modern Art – Sedlmayr found in the art of the preceding century a series of formal characteristics: fragmentation and disjunction, polarisations, shallowness, lack of a sense of a base or ground, and confusion of 'up' and 'down', flight from the organic form, and some other properties in that vein. Then, people's perception of their relations to other people and more particularly to god and nature – this too, he felt, was fragmented and disjointed, polarised into oppositions, shallow, ungrounded and topsyturvy, unorganic. The first set of characters, artistic and formal, was seen as being symptomatic of the second. But to say (for instance) that a pictorial or architectural structure is formally disjointed and then that a person's sense of relation to the human or the divine is as being a disjointed relation was to take 'disjointed' in two different senses. What the two references of the word could have in common – some general formal property of discontinuity – was no basis for deriving one from another. Of course, this can be discussed at other levels – in terms of two realms of *Struktur*, or in terms of mediation – but for me it was a matter of language I found I could not negotiate in a reputable way.

Sedlmayr was a relevant negative for me. What I had known of him before going to Munich had seemed as if it might have some resonances with Leavis: there was cultural critique of post-Industrial Revolution alienations, for instance, and – though the elaborate and explicit procedure was antipathetic – there was close analysis; and, above all, there was a will to apprehend a moral character directly from the manner of a work of art. (This last I still long to do; the matter is not polished off by invoking a Physiognomic Fallacy.) If I had an intention to do anything like Leavis on art this was something to settle with or at least place. But Leavis had analysed voices, as behaviour, and the behaviour was verbal behaviour within and so about a moral and social ambience or frame. There was no such hiatus as that between disjointed forms in art and disjointed views of the world. At Munich that year my sense of Sedlmayr was as a clever man gone astray, flawed, and also as a potentially dangerous man. Later, I came to see him in retrospect as less clever and dangerous than out of his depth.

I say this now. How clear was I about it at the time? I knew all I have just stated much more fully than I do now. What I have just stated is a description of what I knew and thought then, not afterwards, but it has a crispness and thinness, a lack of shading and detail and frayed ends, that my then state of mind did not have.

So I wrote my paper for Ludwig Heydenreich at the Zentral-institut. Heydenreich was a shy and reputedly difficult man who had previously been Director of the German Institute in Florence and was known for his work on Leonardo. His seminar on the Ducal Palace at Urbino, an exercise in how to use documentary sources, was the best formal teaching I had in art history. I particularly recall an hour the dozen of us spent with the ground-plan and the fascinating Urbino staff-list, reconstructing the routes different people would take through or across, or up and down, the central courtyard – what their status and purposes, preoccu-pations and points of view would be. I recall less clearly my own paper on the *studiolo* at Urbino, read late in the summer semester. The afternoon was hot, my paper was long, and a *Turnerfest* or parade of gymnastic clubs was noisily going on outside in the Königsplatz. The Institute is in one of a pair of buildings that had been Party headquarters and for the seminar we sat around a table in a front room giving on to a sort of reviewing balcony or platform. At the height of the drums and bugles and cheering we gave up for a time and went out on the balcony to watch. Eventu-ally we went in again and I finished my piece, but actual memory breaks off at this point.

. . . It does seem to me now that I was being rather easy on myself, writing only the one paper that year, but I was reading widely and attempting to live widely and one time-consuming part of the second I refer back to Christmas at Salzburg. I had arrived in Munich in November for the academic year and rather than going back to Scotland for Christmas went on my own for three or four days to Salzburg: snug hotel, new books, grand masses in the churches, and snowy walks – perfect. At lunch on Christmas day in some beer house up near the Schloss I real-ized that three young American women at the next table were discussing me in an extended way, apropos of their own lack of male companions just now. They assumed I had no English. It was agreed I must be questionable to be alone at such a time and the moustache I had recently grown (intended to be like the actor Anton Walbrook's) was a drawback, but physical possibilities were projected and spun out for some time, particularly by one of them, who had the air of making a hobby of that. I was not attracted, particularly not by her, and at the end of my meal left without making a move, not even the obvious negative one of saying goodbye or merry Christmas in English. But the incident had been objectifying of the self. Hearing oneself assessed as a proposition by three coarse females from another culture sharpens one edge of self-awareness.

Back in Munich after Salzburg I began to feel a lack and became more active about trying to mend it. In both Milan (not Pavia) and St Gallen I had happened on satisfying and easygoing liaisons: I bore no scars from either, nor did anyone else. Munich was more testing, the events in one form or another bathetic. Quite early on, shyly pursuing someone outside my sept and league, I made a fool of myself at the Haus der Kunst, where *Fasching* balls were held; the memory of this is too phantasmagoric to be embarrassing: Caligari at the Blue Angel. But for a different, more representative mess the master-image is a Tyrolese-type hat in Ernst Schnabel's lecture-room. I had met a thin, pale girl at his lectures whom I found waif-like and poignant. I was touched by the anxious intensity on her face when she listened to Schnabel, or to me, and by her sharp starved nose. We had had a few modest meals together and made a modest excursion to the palace at Schleissheim and its then wonderfully neglected gardens, and tonight we were going to have a more ambitious evening after the lecture. The memory is of the horror of seeing her arrive for it in this totally transforming hat – grey felt, green trimming, feathers: cute-*völkisch* – and the shock of revulsion from the thin-lipped striver I now suddenly and unfairly saw.

It was basically a failure of cultural tact, an insensitivity to local signs and systematic associations. An academic year spent in another country does not take one as far into it as one would like to think it is doing. For someone of my sort, part of the problem was that the literature was weak. It is hard to recall now how little of the German literature that achieved a reckoning with 1933–45 was generally current in 1958. The *Gruppe 47* people and others were of course at work but I did not know them. What foreign occasional readers like me knew would be, say, Ernst Jünger, Wolfgang Borchert and Heinrich Böll — to my ear all in different ways questionable, even the gentle flow of fine feeling in the early Böll. This was the year before Günter Grass and *The Tin Drum*, 1959, which marked the opening for a general public of the real campaign, and I did not read that till several years later in London, and then only in English translation.

V
TWO WORKING AMBIENCES
1958–65

I.

It is striking and painful that the mental images of dead friends should be such attenuated images. Presumably the case is much the same as that of absent friends, just more painful. In my experience they usually have an air of sitting and not so much talking as being in talking position, often in a specific but hardly particularized locale, known to one. If one works to retrieve particulars of that locale, one often can do so, but while one is doing so the person fades for a time. There feels to be some functional separation between remembering persons and remembering places. The distance from which one sees the people is variable or even undefined – I do not know which – but the angle has a tendency towards a slightly off-front view of the head. I understand such preferences may be related to angled front views admitting most 'information'. With some effort one can sometimes rotate the head to get, say, a sideways view but I think this is an impoverished, coarse-screen thing. In general the image lacks initiative and visual vitality. It never surprises and it resists yielding detail. Of course, mental imagery is supposed not to be an analogue registration anyway, but rather a coded 'description': but, in this case, description of what? Measurements à la Bertillon or some modification of a geometry-like schema? Propositions about what? And how far are those particulars only an initial prompt for vision-related construction or re-construction into an image?

111

I met Gertrud Bing at the Warburg Institute in London in the early summer of 1958, and so knew her for only six years. There had just been a revolution in Iraq and the job I had lined up for the next academic year after Munich teaching English language at the university in Baghdad had suddenly fallen through. (Baghdad may seem an odd choice even then, but it was connected with plans to spend time also in the Lebanon, still quiet at the time.) At this flat moment Bing took me into the Warburg Institute, more or less off the street, and I really do not know why: I had recently removed my moustache because it made my mother weep, but I know my presence was Ottonian in its blankness. It may be that connection with Ludwig Heydenreich, an old friend of Bing's, had something to do with it. I had written to the Institute from Munich to ask about its research fellowships, though much too late for that year, and she had replied suggesting I come and see her when next in London. I did so and she proposed I work part-time in the photograph library and apply for the next fellowship at the Institute.

(The Warburg Institute had evolved from the private library of Aby Warburg in Hamburg, one element in whose interests as a historian was the sometimes covert after-life of pictorial motifs surviving from pagan antiquity and of energies associated with them. He and his assistant Fritz Saxl developed the library into a more open centre for cultural history, Saxl in effect directing it from the end of the First World War since Warburg was incapacitated for some years by illness. When Warburg died in 1929 Saxl had the support of the Warburg family in maintaining and expanding it. In 1933 it moved from Hamburg to London and in 1944 it became part of the University of London. Saxl died in 1947. Both Warburg and Saxl must in different ways be seen as inspired, perhaps one the more imaginative, the other more pragmatically indomitable. Gertrud Bing had been close to both of them and central to the Institute, Warburg's assistant from

1924 till 1929, Saxl's assistant-director and companion during the difficult transition to England and after. She became Director in 1955, retired in 1959, and died in 1964.)

When Bing died it was a common experience among her friends to realize suddenly that, close to her as they felt, they knew very little about her. Donald Gordon, who had known her since the 1930s and wrote much the best memoir of her – which I should declare I re-read a couple of months ago and intend to play off here – pointed to two aspects of this: one knows and knew almost nothing about her life before she arrived at the Warburg Institute in 1922, aged thirty; and she was someone who kept her separate friendships in separate compartments. One knew she was a Hamburg Bing, a niece of the great art-nouveau dealer Siegfried Bing, that she had been a schoolteacher for a while before writing her Ph.D. thesis on Lessing, and that is practically all. The circumstances and contingencies of her first thirty years must be implicated in the extraordinary strength of the years after. As for the compartmentalizing of her friends, this was the other side of her total focus on the person she was talking with. It was one-to-one with Bing or nothing much, but there must have been a hundred people who enjoyed this sense of her special attention.

Like Gordon, my sense of Bing is particularly attached to evenings spent with her at the house in Dulwich. The house had a strong visual ethos, austerely comfortable and ordered in a taste I thought I recognized, a Germanic cognate of a familiar enlightened Quakerish English taste, but with the strong presence of Saxl through the many small near-eastern objects. Often there were unexpected quirky house-guests, present at dinner but disappearing after: I best remember Hanns Swarzenski, then of the Boston Museum, sober at the time but teased by Bing. The signal that the evening proper was beginning, I came to recognize, was the moment when Bing put aside for a while the last forkful of her dessert and lit a Gauloise. This was an important and clearly cherished moment in the day. Conversation was over and from now on it would be talk. Within a couple of minutes she seemed to modulate into someone different from the twinkling, controlled, adroit institutional person one knew at Woburn Square and became a more private person, of unique experience, both indiscreet and reticent, inquisitive and moody.

Presently, when Bing had finished her dessert, one went up alone with her to the big study, which had once been Saxl's study and contained a number of the small near-eastern objects, though very tidily. Bing sat at the desk – which is where my mental image puts her – oneself in a very German chair, easier than it looked. What followed was not what Gordon tells of getting from Saxl, a tutorial, but a sort of induction by-the-way, an informal indoctrination in a tradition. One talked about people, novels, music, Germany and Italy, very little about England (in which, I agree with Gordon, she was not urgently interested at this time), about Warburg and Saxl, in an un-intense way about life generally, though on that she would sustain a cool tone partly through sub-ironic quotation: as, *erlaubt ist was sich ziemt*, which she said was from Goethe's *Tasso* – what's seemly is all right. One was sometimes very aware that she had begun as a student of the German Enlightenment. She was communicating lore, tales and tips, a morale, and much of it was in the form of a moral placing of people. She was always curious about what one thought of this or that person encountered, particularly German scholars, and when one had committed oneself she would respond. She could convey a quite subtle qualifying view of what one had just said by the timing and pace with which her hand moved the cigarette to her mouth, her face expressionless and unchanging; or she might then throw in some pointed fact about the man's behaviour, or quote Saxl's view of him. What she valued was good people doing good work, but she accepted what there was.

Gordon mentions her capacity for 'scorn' and the word is right, warmer than 'contempt' and admitting humour about the comedy. I remember Kenneth Clark being placed as 'the Toscanini of the diapositives', not praise, yet I know she liked Clark – who, among other things, had spoken up for Warburg's famous overlong Hertziana lecture of 1928.

A few personal loyalties were absolute: above all Warburg (pronounced *Warbur-r-ch*) and Saxl, of course, though the only time she got seriously angry with me was when I said something about the nobility of one of her friend Otto Klemperer's Beethoven performances seeming to me too intentionally noble – a third-rate remark that outraged her. She wrote of Warburg: 'He moved like a man in a dark and dangerous place', and I think the 'moved' is meant literally, of his gait and bearing. She wrote elsewhere of Saxl's 'distrust' of a world he knew to be 'merciless'. To some extent she too moved like someone who had moved through dark and real dangers, but someone who had decided long ago to tough it out. She seemed to travel very resolutely through an only provisionally friendly territory.

Again a photograph intervenes – though there are few photographs of Bing – an extraordinary picture of 1929, the year of Warburg's death, when she would have been thirty-seven. I am sure this is the person I knew in 1960. It is a pair with a well-known last portrait photograph of Warburg in his sitting-room at the Hotel Eden in Rome, taken on the same occasion with the camera identically placed. The small figure of Warburg had been set uneasily in an armchair noisy with brocade and antimacassar, next to a round table, looking warily out left of the camera, and insecurely holding what look like a couple of prints, attribute of the scholar. But Bing's photograph has her sitting up on the arm of the same noisy armchair, which has been moved a few inches leftwards to make space, hands in her lap, no attribute, and legs crossed under the table. She is looking rightwards within the picture space, not outwards left, and wearing what I take to be a gentlewoman's quiet dress but conspicuously elegant shoes. In the left background are shelves with Warburgian-looking books and an index-slip box and such; further across, photographs have been pinned up comparatively on a screen, many of them being photographs of other screens with photographs pinned comparatively on them: Warburg's enterprise. Bing's head is distinguished by the strong jaw and the dark eyes under alert eyebrows, unflinching, formidable and intriguing. I did not know the *ninfa egeria modernissima* the Italian historian Delio Cantimori thought he perceived, and the tone of his remark is surely wrong, but I trust Gordon when he says that, in the late thirties, he saw an 'advanced woman of the twenties'.

I have come across a sheet of pencilled notes she sent me on some piece I had written, about 1960, evidently a paper on Renaissance decorum. I have lost my piece, but her notes on it – densely written in the frugal Institute manner on the back of galley-proof of the British Museum Library supplementary catalogue for 1949 – have something of her voice and her eye for locating the evasive, tricky or self-deceiving. It begins: 'I am always getting a little nervous nowadays when everybody, thanks to Gombrich, talks of relationships.' It ends: 'As to your last sentence, did you not always intend to do that?' Equivocation and *petitio principii* evidently. Though the detailed comment is constructive and encouraging, it was the sharp edge and the candour – real attention – one loved and wanted.

But I bring these notes in here mainly because at one point in them she suddenly asks: 'Is durability not also a moral quality?' The general context is material durability of architecture, and the moral quality is counterposed in a neoclassical pattern with the qualities of being useful and of being pleasing: she is speaking in conformity with a Renaissance pattern of thought. There is an obvious resonance with at least the terms of the 'continuous moral energy' Gordon rightly saw in her. But there are two distinct things in play here, endurance and morality; and on the face of it her question can also be taken in two ways. Is there a moral value in enduring? Is there a moral judgement to be made about the value of any case of survival? She meant the first, and I do think her remark suggests one of her conscious demands of herself, but it is the second her goodwill-with-toughness so satisfied.

Retirement, or at least *Ruhestand*, did not suit Bing. She was worried about the direction in which the Warburg Institute would now go. She was, no wonder, unable to make quick progress with the intellectual biography of Aby Warburg (an almost overdocumented man) that was her project for writing, and in retrospect it was not kind of us her friends to present a frame of easy expectancy. The twinkling persona or mask came more to the fore. After a couple of years, I think (as did Gordon) there was some withdrawal into the German culture and indeed language – again, no wonder. During her last three years I was not at the Institute and saw her only away from it and a final shaming failure is that I cannot remember anything about the talk on the last evening spent with her, just before the illness from which she died. She had come up to Hampstead and left rather late, certainly after one, to drive back to Dulwich. All her friends were uneasy about Bing and the motor car: fortunately she was the sort of bad driver other drivers spot a mile off and avoid. But I was a little anxious when I took her out to her car, since she had drunk a fair amount. She would not stay the night. Somehow we set off her car-alarm, a new-fangled thing neither of us knew how to turn off, and it took time and the pressing help of neighbours before she left for Dulwich, which she safely reached. I was unnerved, she was not.

The backward perspective in which I must see Bing is elaborately foreshortened: there are now forty years back to the six years when I actually knew her; but then there are her twenty-five London years before that, without and with Saxl, then the dozen Hamburg years with and without Warburg, and then the remote and impenetrable first thirty years before. How can one feel, as I do feel, one knew her well? It is tempting to invoke her Warburg Institute here and wonder whether one's long-term engagement with the intellectual apparatus she had devoted herself to made up an extension of engagement with Bing, but this really won't do. Rather, there might on the other hand be a sense in which the Warburg lore itself is foreshortened like one's perspective on Bing, receding into an early twentieth-century German culture one is not equipped to penetrate.

At the time Bing – along with a rather docile selection committee consisting of Arnaldo Momigliano and Anthony Blunt – recruited me to a two-year junior fellowship at the Institute she was in her last year as Director. Ernst Gombrich, her appointed successor, was away at Harvard that year. Back from America, he found himself landed with me not just as a junior fellow for a couple of years but as a pupil. He had mixed feelings about both. At least the topic of my thesis was within his interests. Initially it was a very broad approach to 'Restraint' in Renaissance behaviour, partly prompted by the last part of Heinrich Wölfflin's *Classic Art*: inhibition about bright colours and violent movements, literary and architectural decorum, mathematical proportion, nice manners, vernacular stoicism, *masserizia* – the ethos depicted in the School of Athens. He was a benign supervisor, tolerating flightiness and overambitious initial scope and pointing to particular materials or models that might focus it all down to a viable enquiry. But my adult relation to Gombrich was of a period later than the period of this reminiscence. What belongs here is first encounter with an intellectual climate, the Warburg Institute.

When I first entered the Institute they had just – only a couple of months before, I think – moved from the improvised premises they had had in the Imperial Institute in South Kensington. The new building in Bloomsbury was the worst sort of University of London building, bleak and unthinking, but it was new and theirs, and supposedly made to fit. They had not yet settled in. What I encountered in an oddly unqualified or exposed condition was therefore a couple of dozen people and the books. Say the human nucleus in 1958 was two or three dozen people: one might make it either more or less, according to the matter in hand. Some were on the staff, whose roll I simply call: Gombrich, Kurz, Barb, Trapp, Ligota; Frankfort, Heimann, Webster, Fein; Buchthal, Yates, Mitchell, Ettlinger; Meyer, Rosenbaum, Horstead. Others were not, but long and strongly associated with it. I suppose they fell into five or six classes. There was a small handful of people on the staff who went back to Hamburg days; there were as many who had come from Austria after the move from Hamburg in 1933; there were a few people from an important generation who had had to leave Germany before fully completing their German education; there were English people (Donald Gordon was one) whose research interests were isolated in England and had impelled them to the Institute; and there were Europeans and Americans who came to work when they could, often senior scholars who had known the pre-war Institute. There was also a sixth class of eminent old hands whose relation to the Institute had at some point become tender or problematic: some of these came to the place but some pointedly did not; and one of them intermittently lurked in a nearby tea-room and summoned individuals out to him there. The Institute existed as an interaction of these people with the intention of the books.

When I went to work in the photograph collection in 1958 I was given two successive chores, really conceived to give a grounding in the matter of the Institute. The first was to find alternative subject locations for duplicate illustrations left over from the recent publication of Saxl's *Lectures*. The second was

to gather illustrations for a forthcoming Italian edition of Warburg's Works. (Both these large posthumously published works
were edited by Bing.) It was envisaged that I would not only
read these books but take time to familiarize myself with their
matter and reference, as I did. It was a fine way to approach the
Library. Perhaps I was less grateful for this than I later became.
I could not develop an active interest in astrology, which was the
first classic subject matter of the Institute. Its historical role and
ingenuity were clear: I just had no taste for the areas of mind and
experience on which it bore and drew. A second subject matter of
the Institute was the use by later artists of motifs from classical
art. Again I could see the importance of this but felt no appetite
for working on it myself, as such, though Warburg made it central to Renaissance constraint. None of this mattered because I
was soon captivated by the Library and its frame of mind.

Since this experience is still such a determining element in
what I see as my lamination I am interested in what the mechanics of the process were.

I suppose one way of acquiring a habit of thought is by learning an explicit formal method, and since I like the notion of tidiness I have now and then wished for one of these. But methods
have never worked very well for me because in practice they
have lacked positive purchase on the materials. I have mainly
been aware of method, whatever it may in fact be in this context, as a negative resource or censor: one can have good rules
about things not to do. On the other hand, method implicit in a
body of intellectually consistent particular studies has affected
me much more, even when I was not aware of it as being method
at the time. A third kind of agent is the electrifying individual
concept with systematic corollaries, suddenly making sense of
what one had been vaguely worried about. The case I think of
here is Ernst Gombrich's expansive use of the idea of 'projection', which changed whole provinces of thinking for me.

The Warburg Library itself was a fourth kind. The frame of mind, the intention of the Library, obviously lay in a selection and arrangement of books, in the sense that energy lay in an order of the components. Any one book changes when it is put into any library, due to the other books on the shelf, but more powerfully here by larger-scale patterns and smaller-scale distinctions. I learned how to carry out tasks of enquiry there and this was a matter of learning and using sets of categories and their place in a pattern. With this went certain sequences of reference and relative orientation. One paced all this out physically in the stacks. I think of it now (but did not then) as a little like the training of a neural network or connectionist brain, a developing pattern of associations which experience of successes and failures has habituated one to, a structure of favoured and facilitated moves from one thing to another. At the same time there were functional nodes, shelves which played an organizing part over a wider zone than themselves.

A reader is not passive in a library, of course, and will force transitions it does not prompt or is even obstructive towards, but the presence or absence of a book here or there, or its remoteness or its juxtapositions, accumulatively make up a grain with and against which one habitually works, and by which one may to some extent gauge oneself. In fact the more obvious characteristics of the Warburg Library were not the most powerful: the rigorous separation of Sources from Studies; the east-to-west hierarchy of topographical ordering, which often impinges on temporal ordering; even the four domains realized in the four floors of the Bloomsbury building – social, magical-cum-scientific-cum-religious, literary/literal, visual. Even exotic oddities like the role of the Apperception section were easily discounted. The more powerful pressure came from detailed habits of classification that entailed broad assumptions about how the human world works. This quality is not elusive, just ungainly to describe.

An example then: there was (and, of course, is) a section on German humanists – 'Medieval and Humanistic Literature: Germany' (Sources NAE1 and Studies NAH6000, 2nd floor) – just as there are sections on humanists in other countries. I was told it had been a special care of Hans Meier, an Institute librarian killed in the London blitz, who himself worked in this field. It was a surprisingly small and brilliantly constructed section. It was small partly because Meier had selected very fastidiously only the books, brochures and scruffy offprints that actually did something. There was no academic or celebratory junk here at all: one knew that not to look, at least, at every item would be to deprive oneself. The order in which they were arranged within the section played an idiosyncratic game between topography and chronology, stimulating because non-obvious. I cannot claim to have understood all its implicit rationale of priority, transmission and affinity though there certainly is such.

However, another reason for the section being small is that great masses of German humanism are not in it. To find this and that one is soon impelled across to 'German Literature' and 'Education: Germany', only a few bays away, but also further. Where is Melanchthon, central to German humanism? His works, including his humanistic work on such things as rhetoric and dialectic, are with the Reformers in Religion on another floor (3rd), on which are also Magic and Science, where such humanists as Agrippa von Nettesheim crop up, as both Sources and (separately) Studies. One is referred to Secular Iconography and Dürer's writings and much else down on the Visual floor (1st); and to the Strassburg nationalist historians and the oddly placed 'Rhetoric: Sources' and much else up on the Social Patterns floor (4th). It would be easy to list a couple of dozen other cues regularly met in the German humanism section: – the renaissance of cartography, millennium, Paracelsism, chorography, mining and metals, the Empire, pastoral. . . .

But what is fascinating is that Meier's structured minimalism in the section itself has the effect not of minimizing its part but of installing it as one of many higher-level nodal points in the Library, with an almost generalized force stretching out into many more particularly demarcated activities. It embodies a conception of culture. Culture is made up of ideas, enduring but plastic ideas, formed within both intrinsic and local extrinsic constraints, acting on events, through minds. You pace this out, in the stacks. It becomes part of the armature of knowledge.

An organization of this sort is sensitive to shifts in balance and differentiation. There was a tension between the systematic implication of the core library and the re-balancing entailed in keeping the library alive, in accommodating new books and new interests: clearly it had to evolve and clearly it had been evolving ever since the moment of its first crystallization in Warburg's mind, whenever that quite was. The move to London in 1933 inevitably brought an accelerating normalization towards what one would call anglo-saxon types of focus if that did not beg questions – it became more philological, monographic, institutional, at any rate, and less wild. But the temporal strata in the library are easily sensed, if one wills, and finding one's preferred levels is part of the deal. Myself, I felt particularly at home around 1930.

I wrote practically nothing in the two years of my fellowship since I was fully engaged in reading. I did take notes, some typed and some in an immature hand I cannot now identify myself with, on half-quarto slips of any sort of paper, organized into cardboard boxes – a broadly Warburg-like behaviour.

2.

Since encounter with the Warburg Library was what mainly formed me, this might seem the moment to stop – snugly berthed for a while. But for reasons that may or may not become clear I feel an impulse to disorder the narrative and let in some contradictions and tensions. And I think I can do this by admitting proleptically a few motifs from the three or four years that followed that first sojourn in the Warburg Library. They may throw a back light.

I have not mentioned that during these early years in London I lived at the top of a four-storey mews house in Chelsea – Bury Walk behind Sidney Street. I looked out and down on to a minute crenellated house called The Gothic Box, inhabited by a fringe art-world figure called Simon Neighbour or Simon Gentleman or perhaps Simon Messenger, I cannot remember which, and also on an uncrenellated small house lived in by a sister of the good Australian actor Peter Finch, who now and then gave good late-night drunken performances in the street when she would not let him in. My landlady, Constance Howard, was a textile artist who had been one of the Whitchurch regulars before the war. Her husband Harold Parker was a versatile sculptor, as sculptors need to be, designer of the wren on the reverse of the farthing but also of superior crash-helmets. His studio was in Camden Town, Connie's in the house, though she was heavily engaged at Goldsmiths' College at New Cross, where she built up the school and centre of textile art now named after her. I do not actually remember her at Whitchurch as an individual, only her dog Doggy Jim, but if I were choosing one object to suggest the Whitchurch aesthetic it might well be an engraving I have by Connie of Susannah and the Elders in modern dress, 1939, a nocturne reeking of period. They were delightful people and I am sure I was benefitting undeservedly from Connie's wish to make return to my parents.

I have already tried twice to think about memory of a miscellaneous iterative texture – Manchester and St Gallen – so it is not to the purpose to describe general London life of those years, but I will mention that Bury Walk was extraordinarily well placed for it. It was only one long block away from South Kensington tube and a generous range of buses, including the 14 for Bloomsbury.

And it was only a step further to the Victoria & Albert Museum with the National Art Library, where I read regularly during my first year in London. I was still in Bury Walk in 1961, when I joined the staff of the V&A as Assistant Keeper (Second Class) in the Sculpture Department. My office was hardly ten minutes' walk away.

In the Sculpture offices at the south-east corner of the Museum we were seven: John Pope-Hennessy, Terence Hodgkinson (later Director of the Wallace Collection and Editor of the *Burlington Magazine*), the medievalist John Beckwith, the senior museum assistant Len Joyce, two museum assistants who changed rather often through promotion, and myself. There were three ways in or out.

The first way was by a large elevator that sometimes carried crates up a couple of floors to the Department of Ceramics but also went down to a semi-basement where my own office was, away from the others, next to a store-room in which small sculpture was kept. I liked my office, new-built when I arrived. It looked out southwards on a wall of the dry moat that separates the V&A from the Cromwell Road but was secluded, fresh and bigger than the others, and fitted out with surprisingly attractive Edwardian office furniture retrieved from obsolete stock. I particularly enjoyed my second desk, a tall desk with a wide and deep sloped top and big level wings on each side, designed for someone sitting on a high stool but good for standing to work with big catalogues, such as Habicht's marvellous corpus of German Renaissance medals. It was a cheerful room except on a few sunny summer afternoons, when some combination of light angles and heavily leafed plane-trees on the street above could make one feel stowed away. In the lobby outside there was an almost private door opening on to a deserted Far Eastern gallery, just next to a brassy Javanese gamelan, and this gallery led one quietly west towards the museum main entrance.

The second way out was through the Sculpture Department waiting-room, where on two or three afternoons a week my duty as junior keeper was to attend on any visitors wanting advice on Objects. No one positively liked this duty, which fragmented time and was a tie, but such visitors were far fewer in Sculpture than in Ceramics, who had a hard time at it upstairs. The skills were primitive: avoiding valuation; assuring oneself the thing was really theirs and not on approval from a dealer who would sue; assuring the visitor that while it might not be 'rare' in the understood sense of worth much, yet it was surely a nice thing to possess and enjoy for itself. There was a low-grade craftsman's pleasure in sending people off content. What went down best was the illustrated catalogue of the great Fonderie Italiane Riunite, Naples; they could see there their reproduction antique statu-ette available in 1900 with a choice of three different patinations, black, brown or green. Neatness eased any disappointment.

The outer waiting-room door opened on to the study collec-tion of sculpture. On the right, Renaissance medals and plaquettes recently reordered and re-labelled by myself; on the left, Renais-sance bronze statuettes in expensive new cases designed by John Pope-Hennessy to house the things too high for the other half-dozen bronze statuette experts to see. They were small men as a class, though it might be, as John Beckwith claimed, that it was one particular American scholar he had in mind. This room led to the front of the museum.

The third way out, often taken several times a day, leading north to the library and the centre of the museum, began by go-ing up perhaps seven or eight steps. Then, passing the top of a dark staircase that went down to the Oratory-side staff entrance and *conciergerie*, where morning and evening one collected and surrendered keys, it became a very long corridor running at last to a door giving on the galleries. I cannot now usefully estimate its length in yards and have no clear visual memory of the placing of the big windows along the left side or the outlook – though I think this was on to low roofs – but on the right were a whole series of doors, first rooms of the Textiles people, then of the Director's offices. Along its whole length the floor was polished brown lino.

Starting out one day from the south end I saw John Pope-Hennessy (who will be my representative V&A figure) starting from the north. Encounters with people here were of course routine but I had noticed an awkwardness about them both in myself and in others. The long approach toward another person down this stark perspective gave too much time, so that one found oneself actually making a decision about at what point to give the collegial smile or nod or whatever one was going to do in that line. Too early was inane and too late was off-hand. One does not usually ponder these things: people lost spontaneity in the corridor. Meanwhile Pope-Hennessy was closing.

He was a fast walker but not lithe. He didn't quite coast along but his wasn't a stride formed by, say, a habit of rough shooting over plough and tussocks. It was a smooth urban gait of a kind one often sees on the longer crosstown blocks in New York, in fact, but fast. Perhaps four yards away he looked at me and opened his peculiar mouth as preparing to speak about something, and veered a degree in my direction. I slowed and, I suppose with a yard or two to go, halted to receive his communication, and without breaking step or losing speed he swerved slightly round me and went on his way without a word. I was left standing, foolish.

I found the incident interesting because it displayed in such a pure and innocent form an impulse behind much of his behaviour. He was playful and he liked to win even when he had rigged the game. (Obviously, even if I had known he was going to do what he did, perhaps from previous experience, I couldn't have passed on: that would have left him an opening for being outrageously ignored. It is a game white can always win.) But, really, for him the preliminary setting up of a rigged game was the game. He often became bored with actually playing it through. On the other hand again, if the rigging somehow came unstuck during the playing and he had to improvise, he was stimulated and pleased. The games, if not precisely about power, were at least framed as play exercise towards a position of control.

I had first come into touch with him as a translator, back in 1959 or 1960. He had wanted someone to do translations of the Italian and Latin texts and documents in his good three-volume book on Italian High Renaissance and Baroque Sculpture. He asked Bing, who had proposed me, and I had done them, glad of the money. I met him for discussions a couple of times at and after lunch in his house off Kensington Church Street and at some point he suggested I apply for the new Assistantship coming up in his department in a few months. He had been lively to work for and I decided to try it. I would need a job after the Warburg fellowship. There were three things I did not know. One was that there was someone already in the Museum who wanted the job and had earned it on merit. Another was that I would not be doing serious work on the great Italian collection: a grand catalogue was already in proof. The third was that he would in the mean time fix on yet another young man met somewhere whom he preferred to me. I learned years later from someone who was there that he had fought hard for this person, as a minority of one on the appointment committee but with the weight of Keeper, and it took the insistence of the Civil Service Commission member to get me in.

Given that, he behaved well. It helped that for my first year he was away in America, based in some comfortable eastern university – Smith, Brown or Williams – and snugly holed up ('a little white house with a little black maid') writing his weak book on Raphael. And when he got back to London there were only two years before he knew I would presently be leaving. He left me much time for my own work. The chores he did give me were reasonable and educational. The main one was to draft, on the basis of the new catalogue, new labels for all the nine hundred pieces of Italian sculpture, each with a few lines summing up the essential information on the object – a job to learn from. We had no real spats. He considered my worst deficiency to be in a lack of acquisitiveness on the Museum's behalf, not attending enough to what was at the dealers' and in the sale rooms: but he told me so with good humour and in any case was right.

I liked him and admired his vitality, and found him more interesting than many of his books. I studied his techniques of getting through formidable amounts of work in a short time, though I have not been able to adopt them. I was never witness of one of his atrocities. People I trusted did witness them and I cannot dispute they happened. They seem to have been sudden acts of cruelty or of disloyalty, wilful and ruthless but somehow casual, like some awful child. My experience was that he was not vindictive. Someone, probably John Beckwith, pointed out that Keepers either came to resemble their Objects or chose to curate Objects that resembled themselves. Delves Molesworth of Woodwork was of some battered but good hardwood, Charles Oman of Metalwork was as close to being silverware as a person could be, Wingfield-Digby of Textiles was certainly some very fine stitch, and John Pope-Hennessy was a disquieting Quattrocento pagan putto, bronze.

No doubt he had always been a handful, but I still see him as partly a victim of his own myth in the Museum, where he had been too long. His identity had to some extent become an artefact of the place. Big institutions need and elect a sacred monster and five hundred people there were waiting for him to behave outrageously, and every now and then he did so. I got tired of people in the rest of the Museum waiting, with a sort of furtive glee, for tales of fresh horrors from 'The Pope' – which in fact I could not provide. Among the younger assistant keepers I used to eat lunch with I tried to replace the name 'The Pope' with the more wholesome 'Topsy' but it did not take. In the Department he was 'John', but there the trouble was a sort of cosy domination which the staff colluded with.

The one time in the day all four keepers met was Tea, a little before five in John's room. A museum assistant brought jasmine tea and very sweet cake got from the Brompton Road. Three of us, plus any casuals, sat round John at his desk and exchanged information, gossip and wit. Even a grammar-school lad could see this was study tea with Captain-of-Bobs or some such person and the last straw was when the most regular of the casuals, M. of Painting, was there to add in his half-broken voice a mix of scandal – this was Profumo and Stephen Ward time among other things – and flattery. Terence Hodgkinson, laconic and reserved, represented the better element, with whom I associated myself; and John Beckwith – who, I kept in mind, had been badly wounded in Normandy on D-day + 1, which was much more than I could claim – flattered and quipped. John Pope-Hennessy presided, occasionally dismissive but basically liking it all. I took to going late.

On rare occasions when I came up from my semi-basement to Tea I found John alone, the other two both off somewhere. Tea à deux followed. He was likely to begin one of his games and the very square high-ceilinged office became a squash court in which he would do all the serving. For instance, I recall him setting out to induce me, if not to say, then to agree – or, at the very least, to allow – that Y., the companion of our mutual friend X., was bad for X. 'A drain on him, don't you think really?' The stakes were high since X. had been a sponsor of mine and though John had known him longer I was now the closer to X.; also I liked

Y. 'So demanding and silly!' Any disloyalty, one wrong smile, would rot my sense of relation to X. and weaken my independence vis-à-vis John himself. 'Has to spend evenings with those people from Cork Street.' I stodgily countered about one point in three and was unresponsive to the other two, which involved being no fun at all, a serious fault, but was just enough to stay on my feet, I hope, though I am not certain. 'Surely you find the eye-shadow appalling?'

'The fuss about getting to the right music festivals!' After some minutes of this he suddenly switched, bored. I may be conflating two separate occasions but I think it was on this occasion that he switched to the Calcagni.

'It's really rather a scandal you've done nothing about publishing the Calcagni', he said.

A couple of months earlier a dealer had brought in a bust, an odd composite affair, bronze head and variegated marble shoulders and pedestal, and a black cartouche with the name of Annibal Caro, the sixteenth-century writer. 'Della Porta!', John had said firmly and a day or two later I had gone off to the Warburg Institute library to see if there was anything of interest to be found at the Caro end. The library at once produced the inventory of Caro's house in Civita Nuova, tidily printed in the back of a modern study of the man, with the bust unmistakeably listed as in the Sala in 1578; and then Filippo Baldinucci's famous 'Notices of Exponents of Design' stating a century later but irrefutably that the bust still in Caro's house was an early work by Antonio Calcagni. That is, not Della Porta. (I shall not develop the art-historical implications: they were not staggering.) When I delivered this and some other stuff about later ownership John was a little miffed but the bust, which we were buying, became 'the Calcagni'.

'I've had to do it myself', he went on now. 'I'm putting it in *Apollo*.'

It had not occurred to me to publish it. I did not even like the bust. The documentation had been neat, but that was a function of Caro's eminence and the right library; and the devilling principle is established in the civil service. In any case it seemed to me a bit early to publish: one or two things about the bust, particularly the variegated marble, which I had noted in an old sale catalogue being called Sicilian, were worth a bit more work.

He was watching closely for reaction. I was always slow to spot the kind of game being played and at first thought it was all simply a way of telling me from strength that he was publishing the bust, which was fine by me. Then I realised it was rather that he was trying actually to induce resentment about him publishing: having been so boring about X., I was now to be stung by a sense he was doing me down over the bust. I did not feel this, and yet this present telling shows he won. I do not recall how the rest of that session went, but what has prompted me to remember this much of it is, among a few other V&A papers I kept two sheets of the slick, signeted, yellowish foolscap used in the Museum for informal drafts, the carbon copy of the Calcagni texts I had delivered. The only possible reason I could have kept these useless sheets is that, when the article appeared, it really was irritating to read the narrative of the author's poised attribution to Calcagni and effortless confirmation by reference to recondite texts. I still keep the sheets.

(My last encounter with John Pope-Hennessy, a good twenty years later at I Tatti in the 1980s, after he had retired to Florence, did not disrupt my sense of him. In the mean time he had been Director of the V&A and of the British Museum in fairly quick order and then had been something I never quite understood at the Metropolitan Museum of Art in New York, but I cannot remember any real encounter during that time. I was due to give the first paper on the second day of a small conference and during the preliminary hanging about before the start of it I was astonished to see him arrive. He was not attending the conference. 'I've come quite especially to hear you', he told me with much of the old top spin, and I still certainly knew better than to take this as a compliment. I made some lame remark about being afraid he would find my paper 'irritating', forgetting that to irritate is to exert a sort of power, and we made mellow conversation for a time. In fact, the paper – a rather artificial argument about limits for the semiotic interpreting of Annunciation pictures – was much more sure to bore him. I gave it, very aware of his poker-faced presence though also having to notice fidgets among the grouped French semioticians. Afterwards it was a few minutes before we could have a word together and he waited, having something to say. 'It didn't irritate me at all', he told me in his unaccented way, when we were able to speak, and then he left, clear winner. It hadn't irritated *him* . . . ? It hadn't *irritated* him . . . ? *It* hadn't irritated him . . . ?)

I was an Italianist but, since the grand catalogue of the Italian collection had just been completed by John Pope-Hennessy and Ronald Lightbown, other work had to be found for me and I was allotted as my main charges the German objects, which I knew nothing about. The most coherent of these objects as a group, I felt, were the late-gothic and renaissance south-German sculptures, a small but good collection, and I set about equipping myself to catalogue them. At that time the Museum considered it one of its functions to enable its staff to become 'authorities', as a public resource: it supported travel for study and contact with museum officials abroad; the National Art Library was a hundred yards from my office, and I could have Veit Stoss's boxwood *Virgin and Child* on my desk while I worked on it. It was a perfect position for getting a grasp of a new field. By the time I left the Museum in 1965 I had a first draft of a small catalogue, eventually published. This is now thoroughly superseded by Norbert Jopek's catalogue of 2002.

I should have got further than that but I had been baffled by the sculpture, by the twirly drapery and pseudo-*contrapposto* and the rest, which I could not place and was not at all sure I liked. The little I wrote for publication on German sculpture at that time was on later Italianate work. I was puzzled by what the sculptors of 1480–1530 could have thought they were doing and spent time finding out a little about their environment – as a matter of curiosity rather than method – and trying to work out a way to think about them: the concepts of the basically Franco-Italianate critical language I knew clearly would not do. After a couple of years I had come to like the sculpture and had in mind some sort of general study. Now and then I have wondered why I left the V&A with so little hesitation. It was a decent life. Mornings I wrote letters and drafted labels and did whatever other Department jobs were outstanding. Lunch, usually with a colleague, I was encouraged to extend by visiting an exhibition or a dealer. (Sculpture is a field in which dealers are likely to be scholarly and interesting.) Afternoons I devoted to my Germans, on the whole. In my own time I was beginning to publish articles on the Italian humanists. I travelled a lot. Why leave? I think I would have said at the time I felt in a false position. The coordinates of a false position – what facts of the environment are rejected by what aspects of oneself – invite a sort of immunology of the self.

Emblematic of the false position for me at the V&A was the EDO. An EDO – which I think stood for Estate Duty Order – was an expertise of objects for which the owners were claiming exemption from estate duty on the grounds that they were 'of national etc. importance', the etcetera taking in artistic or historical interest. The experts were taken from the national museums and as junior man in Sculpture I tended to be the nominee for miscellaneous post-classical sculpture. One was provided with an inventory that gave descriptions and valuations, both of which were to be scrutinised and, if necessary, revised. The description was often that provided by a dealer who had sold the object to the owner and it could be overambitious. The valuations were derivatives from those done for probate and estate duty and were often too low. The third decision was about the national etc. importance or otherwise, yes or no, and this was complicated by a gradual devaluation of the standard, so that often the objects were a second generation bunch being claimed as an addition to unambiguously good stuff approved years ago.

The first general rub was a straight professional incompetence. Often there was sculpture of kinds I knew nothing about, and even when I did know enough about it to have views on a description I was likely to be at a loss about value. I had to bluff and pick colleagues' brains. A second rub was that the fee one was paid for this work was calculated as a proportion of the value one set on the objects. When I saw colleagues coolly raising the valuations on their lists by a factor of three or four I was in no position to have a view about whether they were right or wrong, but some narrow north-country money puritanism was uncomfortable. The third was a social awkwardness. The basic position was ambiguous between being something like a bailiff's man, as the butler at Hinchingbrooke certainly saw me, and an antiquary who has been good enough to drop in with advice, as with the nice people at Knole.

A composite group-visit EDO: one arrives at the train and finds that the three colleagues going on this trip are people one reckons a knowledgeable clown, a knowledgeable spiv, and a decent and knowledgeable man who seems to live in some remote zone otherwise occupied only by his objects. It is not a group one wants to identify oneself with. The collection to be seen today is parvenu, and the Edwardian house near Henley or Hayward's Heath is glossily unsympathetic. So are the collections, which consist of objects in half-a-dozen categories and, at least in the case of my stuff – say English alabasters or eighteenth-century terracottas – have the uniform look of things bought from the same dealer and worked over by the same restorer. They are not fakes but are over-improved and over-supplemented. Getting to work, the clown is soon dropping things with clangs in the next room, the spiv apparently making a general inventory of the house for some purpose of his own, and the decent man is looking at his objects and sighing. The widow arrives with a forty-ish smoothie who is introduced as the son of the dealer who supplied the sculpture; now head of the firm, he has come to offer any collateral information I may need, as he puts it. He hangs around, enthusing about bad objects, and, though nothing is said directly, one begins to sense some old antagonism between him and the spiv, whom I would actually like to be pumping about my valuations but cannot. At lunch nobody but the dealer has much to say; to the widow we are clearly an uncouth intrusion. As is usually the case with sculpture, I have fewer items to deal with than the others and after lunch make moves to order a cab for an earlier train. But the dealer too wants to get back to Town and insists on giving me a lift in his Bentley. En route there is no attempt to nobble, just the creation of a good atmosphere I shall be caddish to disrupt with my report. As we crawl through the traffic of outer London, myself a little nauseous from all the braking on the soft-hard suspension, I notice the hostile looks for us Bentley folk from the people queueing for buses in the rain.

I found it hard to like the institutional quality of life at the V&A. There were hours to keep, casually implemented but represented in principle by a small pink booklet in which one was supposed to note times of arrival and departure for monthly checking of the total. The physical fabric of institutions, here the brown lino and general Ministry of Works tat and botch, can be lowering when one is already low-spirited. I was usually a little depressed by the moment of entry into the Museum, the big human mechanism with its keys and variously unpleasant floors. It felt a little like going to school.

The first decisive thing, however, was my realising, once I got down to the serious business of working on my objects, that I lacked one necessary talent of connoisseurship. It was not that I did not enjoy and esteem connoisseurship. Getting a grasp of a field was in itself very satisfying and a couple of good identifications I made showed me that these offer a pleasure of discovery as pure as one can hope for in a historical activity; I have seen a German connoisseur six feet six inches in height jump with joy in the basement store-room of the V&A when he identified a boxwood statuette as by someone who interested him and I know how he felt.

The talent I lacked was a strong visual memory. The identifications I succeeded in making mostly involved finding a text that described or otherwise identified the object I was starting from. The real connoisseur identifies an object through its visual relation to other objects, which come to his mind when he sees the first. This is the essential act of the connoisseur. Perhaps various kinds of construction and confirmation follow, and there are various different kinds of possible relation which have to be sorted out, but the indispensible basis is that when you see object A, object B – the right object B – comes to mind from your past. For this you need a retentive and ordered visual memory. I think of this talent as distinct from having what is known as 'an eye', which is surely an ability to distinguish an object of quality out of the mass. The two are not unrelated and may coincide in the same person but often do not. John Pope-Hennessy, for instance, certainly had 'an eye' but did not have a particularly good visual memory. He noticeably preferred to work on a project whose visual range could be covered by half-a-dozen illustrated books on his desk, as prompts.

My weak visual memory became particularly clear to me after the study trips I was sent on abroad. I would go off for a month in my newly bought old Volkswagen to Burgundy and Germany or Poland and Czechoslovakia and systematically scrutinise sculpture in museums and churches and occasionally palaces and town squares. On such a trip I would look at a hundred pieces with a particular purpose or pre-existing question in mind and another thousand with more general attention, as part of the repertory. I prepared for this with handbooks and made notes and some sketches and photographs of detail en route. I also made conscious efforts to memorise. A few weeks after I had got back to London the particularity of the visual forms of most of what I had seen had faded away or thickened into a generic porridge. I could not recall how the drapery went on the left flank of a figure seen in Karlsruhe which had come to mind as somehow like the figure in the V&A I was now trying to place. I would go to the library for an illustration and find that the left flank of the Karlsruhe figure was not like that of my figure; and perhaps that there was some other un-significant similarity – say a certain frequency of folding on the under-tunic – that might have set off an association; and perhaps also that the illustration really didn't match my memory of the figure in general effect either. I may have made too much of this. Certainly it was only part of the point of the trips: the physical realities of facture and ambience were also important to study, not to mention the local art historians. But I knew people who demonstrably did retain and retrieve as I did not.

The other element first emerged quite early, at the time when I was being taken around to meet the curatorial staffs of the other departments, one department at a time. There was an elderly and near-retired assistant keeper in one of them, famously disaster-prone, who greeted me warmly. 'It seems no time at all', he said, 'since I used to eat luncheon with your grandfather.' My paternal grandfather died when I was five and I have and had no memory of him. I was already aware that I was following my father in working in an art museum but I had not fully registered that there was a third-generation pattern too. It became a worry.

Family history beyond what one has oneself experienced is, in my view, likely to be a source of false identity. I would leave it entirely aside, except that one's derivation (or what one has taken it to be) may have been part of a sense of environment now and then and to that extent of one's experience. Mine is in any case commonplace and generally uninsistent – farmers and small entrepreneurs, with some later nineteenth-century scattering into various new kinds of activity then opening up. Because the name is odd – probably just a mis-spelling of the common Baxendale but possibly something to do with seventeenth-century Norwegian immigration into Yorkshire – the Baxandall line has been worked and can stand for all.

My immediate paternal line goes: Abraham, Abraham, Jonathan, Jonathan, David, David, David my father. (I see that the American line of Lee Baxandall, the student of Marxist aesthetics and specialized beaches, intersects at the first Jonathan and has the advantage of Phineas as a family name.) The Abrahams and Jonathans had been developers of coal-pits in the West Riding since the first half of the eighteenth century – I hope without child labour. They got by, it seems, since they went on leasing land and extracting for at least a hundred years, but there is no sign of serious long-term accumulation. The first David, my great-grandfather, began in coal too but in the 1860s broke away and became a corn-miller at Ingrow in the Worth Valley, above Keighley: Bronte country. Seen in late photographs taken by my grandfather he is a formidable thick-set square-bearded man, quite interesting. He was a Methodist lay preacher.

My grandfather, the second David, was the youngest of this miller's eleven children. He grew up at the mill, which was converted to steam power but still had its original mill-pond. I am vague about what the older sons did except that one went to sea and was killed in Valparaiso harbour. Of the four daughters two married farmers and the other two were trapped in the role of helpmate to widowed brothers. I allow myself a pang over the fact that none of the children stayed at the mill. Of the three youngest sons – who stayed in close touch with each other – one prospered by writing successful algebra textbooks: I liked and visited his daughter in Surrey. The next became an astronomer at Cambridge and I knew his daughter too. (I was told in childhood two things about him that I remembered: he wore blue-tinted spectacles so as not to attract attention, and he died young from a heart attack after bicycling too vigorously to avoid a person he disliked.) My grandfather David, finally, was a historian of mathematical and astronomical instruments.

He had been trained as a mathematician at the Imperial College of Science but became a keeper at the Science Museum, round the corner from ICS and across Exhibition Road from the V&A – with which (looking at the sorts of instrument he worked on) he would have had in common at least an interest in antique brasswork. He had been a good scholar, I had gathered, and when I now looked at his publications I was impressed. Among other things he was ahead of his time in working on Babbage and early computing. (His 1926 catalogue of the calculating machines in the Science Museum was re-issued with additions in 1975 – good going.) But there seemed to me something unbearably fusty about my own position as third-generation museum custodian. This became an obsession. An existential leap or at least shuffle was due. For this as well as more positive reasons, when Ernst Gombrich wrote proposing I go back to the Warburg Institute permanently, in the first instance to teach rhetoric and dialectic, I did not hesitate.

The ten years I had allowed myself after Cambridge had run out during my last year at the V&A. There was no novel. Here I shall stop.

VI
CODA

Quis, quid, ubi, quibus auxiliis, cur, quomodo, quando?

The project in this writing was to feel the way to a rhetoric of recall. I wanted to locate forms or templates that intervene in our recollection of the past, partly so that they could be allowed for in self-critically viewing the past.

What I have to say about the rhetoric of the remembered self I have, after a fashion, said – I find.

It is implicit in the individual pieces of reminscence to which this text has constantly reverted.

I had intended something more analytical, in which the pieces of actual reminiscence would exemplify types and structures. Instead, whenever I set about putting down a piece of exemplary stuff, its independent demands and energy took over. Looking back, this has been the case at least since the story of Godwin. From the third chapter on I was following where the tale took me.

As I made an initial point about not writing memoirs, there is some awkwardness here, but I shall ignore it.

In fact, looked at as rhetoric, this has invited a rhetoric in the middle range or scale – not the grand rhetoric of a whole or its structure, and not the local rhetoric of the individual figure of speech or thought, but an intermediate level of discursive schemes that may underlie a passage of one paragraph or twenty. (In classical rhetoric the similarity in scale would be with the *Progymnasmata* but there is only limited overlap with the particulars of these and I shall not pursue this relation.)

Most of what I have written has fallen into half a dozen different types of discourse, often interwoven with, or subordinated to, one of the others. The main types I discern are:

141

    i   sub-narrative vignettes
   ii local narratives of an episode
  iii synthetic general accounts of the texture of an everyday
  iv sketches of persons
   v evocations of places
  vi reductions of states of mind and feeling to rational summary

But of course what I have written was often intended to exemplify such types, as a succession of set pieces with short bridge passages, and there is little interest in the degree of their conforming with the typology. The interest is in their individual forms and burden.

The process of memory – from the conditioned firing of some synapses in the brain to the writing by St Augustine of his Confessions – is long and multifacetted and has many moments and liaisons. The moment I envisage here – which in this chapter I shall refer to as *'recall'* – is one of purposeful and directed address to the memory, of deliberately casting the mind back. Its product is more crystallized than the fluid stuffs we meet more passively in reverie, say, which is a moment preceding recall.

Much of its agenda is summed up in the Latin hexameter that is the title of this chapter: who, what, where, by aid of what, why, how, where? Persons, things, places, instruments, causes, manners, moments.

The product is edited: selected and ordered.

Here is one of the points of strain.

Fragmented, summary, selective, confined.

What is the relation of these formally written-up pages to the more fluid stuff of reverie and introspection and sense of self? The pages are more crystallized and dedicated to covering some selected matter. At the same time they are lacking in an assumed field of available contextual reference. When I happen on Godwin's village during some reminiscence I do not rehearse 'stone-built farms' and 'horse-pond' and so on in my mind; but I have a global sense of the village, not necessarily focussed and certainly not total recall, but certainly including the pub and the shop and Dai Lloyd's braces and much else not cited in the script. I may refer to any or all this or I may not, but it is accessible and it is assumed.

Much depends on what is supplied.

Vignettes and episodes seem defined by difference from each other, the vignettes resisting narrative whereas episodes do not. I made a point of vignettes such as sitting in the trap in the early morning dark having great power in one's memory but they are not what Lessing called pregnant moments and I am not sure that they even represent one occasion. They feel much more like metaphors in that their significance

NARRATION

We have been trained by parents or others to produce local narratives of ourselves from an early age – 'What have you been doing?', or the more loaded 'Did you have a good time?' – and apparently parents who offer good models of narration produce children who narrate well, good performance having been rewarded with attention and approval.

At the centre of our difficulty in recalling the past accurately is a mismatch between what we want and the equipment we must use to achieve it. What we may suppose we want is something like a narrative chronicle but one in which, having found our place, we can refer to people and places, incidents and textures of life, in close focus. We accept that this chronicle has gaps and foggy areas, distortions and misproportions

An expanded and humanised curriculum vitae with optional links offering enlargements and additions in all directions

The equipment with which we attempt this has evolved towards other functions, including

Conceptualization, which is generalization and not favourable to individualizing detail

Prototypes, schemata, integration, inference, background information

SELF

Attention to one's own past attention.

The writing of a sort of narrative has persuaded me that the self is not a narrative we live by, as has been attractively argued.

One of the established issues about the 'self' is whether, or how far, it is something constructed through a process of narration: we would create our identity by telling ourselves about it, rather like a story, mainly about the past but sometimes with projections into the future. This construction would be involved in our self-assessment. A strong version of this has us actively and consciously living out the story at the same time. There are problems about the idea and 'narrative' seems an awkward word for what is going on. But a narrating posture inevitably enters into recovery and rehearsal of the past self.

A more productive issue lies in the status of 'narrative' or 'narration'. Much of the disagreement about how far we construct our self as a narrative comes from fairly obvious equivocation. Narratologists distinguish something like three main senses of narrative/narration (or *récit*). There is (1) a sequence of actions and events that is the object of telling; there is (2) a told sequence of actions and events; and there is (3) the telling, itself a sort of action – as it might be (1) the Trojan War, (2) the Iliad, and (3) Homer singing.

I feel as if what was meant to be a visit to the past has provoked an unexpected return visit in which my past is eyeing me. There is my gimcrack reconstruction of parts of it, but through chinks in this a stranger or strangers, an earlier self or earlier selves, are peering out at me, resentful. I have failed to instal them. Nothing but a laborious recording of every detail I can make myself remember would satisfy and this I do not intend. Yet it is true that every now and then I meet some fragment of memory that is not compatible with the self constructed in this account and suddenly then I lose confidence in that self.

Publisher's note

The final manuscript of this book was approved by Michael Baxandall before his death. A few small emendations have been made for publication. Evidently the Coda is the mind continuing to work on the form of the completed text. Certain repetitions and obscurities have been omitted.

The original typescript is in the Cambridge University Library with the Baxandall Papers.